Jenny Diski was born in 1947 in London, where she lived and worked most of her life. She is the author of nine novels, of which *After These Things* is her most recent; a collection of short stories and two books of essays, including *A View From The Bed and Other Observations*; and two bestselling memoirs, *Skating to Antarctica* (winner of the MIND Book Award) and *Stranger on a Train* (winner of the J.R. Ackerley Prize for Autobiography and the Thomas Cook Travel Book Award). She now lives in Cambridge.

'An original and striking memoir, cool but authentic, filled with emotional imagery and insight that is all the more resonant for its restraint.' – *Independent on Sunday*

'Jenny Diski's *Skating to Antarctica*, part traveller's tale, part autobiography, tells the story of a trip to Antarctica, interwoven with reminiscences of her dysfunctional family and her daughter's quest to find what became of Diski's own long-lost mother. There are great descriptions of penguins and elephant seals and Diski's fellow travellers, and a gripping account of Diski's amazingly awful parents. Keeps you appalled and enthralled.' – *Observer*

'. . . unfailingly sharp-edged prose, confession with its wit about it.' – *Times Literary Supplement*

'*Skating to Antarctica* is a fascinating, moving account of two voyages . . . Diski's book shines out for its wit, lack of self-pity and strong interest in survival. I relished her sketches of ship routine, solemn penguins and bored soldiers . . . Diski has a great sense of the absurd, whether she is writing about her conman father or the sexual antics of an elephant seal. Antarctica is not barren after all.' – Helen Dunmore, *Express*

Also by Jenny Diski

Skating to Antarctica

Jenny Diski

Virago

A *Virago* Book

First published in Great Britain by Granta Books in 1997
This edition published by Virago Press in 2005

A CIP catalogue record for this book
is available from the British Library.

ISBN 1 84408 151 6

Typeset in Horley by M Rules
Printed and bound in Great Britain
by Clays Ltd, St Ives plc

Virago
An imprint of
Time Warner Book Group UK
Brettenham House
Lancaster Place
London WC2E 7EN

www.virago.co.uk

'I wonder if I am not talking
yet again about myself. Shall I be
incapable, to the end, of lying on
any other subject?'

Malone Dies

For Chloe without whom

I am not entirely content with the degree of whiteness in my life. My bedroom is white: white walls, icy mirrors, white sheets and pillowcases, white slatted blinds. It's the best I could do. Some lack of courage – I wouldn't want to be thought extreme – has prevented me from having a white bedstead and side-tables. They are wood, and they annoy me a little. Opposite my bed, in the very small room, a wall of mirrored cupboards reflects the whiteness back at itself, making it twice the size it thought it was. Some time ago, I had a builder in to make another room. He wanted to know what I was going to do with the walls. White, I told him, like the walls throughout the flat. 'I suppose it stops arguments about what wallpaper to have,' he said unenthusiastically. It was the only good reason he could think of for having white walls.

In the morning, if I arrange myself carefully when I wake, I can open my eyes to nothing but whiteness. The soft white of the sheet, with darker white shadows in the folds of the duvet. A brasher white with scored lines at the point where the walls meet the ceiling or turn the corner: ninety-degree angles in shades of white. A repetition of white when I raise my eyes

1

slightly to the mirror opposite. Morning moments of indescribable satisfaction. Eventually, I'll have to let colours in to my day, but for a while I can wallow in a seemingly boundless expanse of white.

If I trace it back, that wish for whiteout began with the idea of being an inmate in a psychiatric hospital. Not during my first stay in a mental hospital, in Hove, when I was fourteen, but later, aged twenty and twenty-one, in London's Maudsley psychiatric unit, hospital became my preferred environment. White hospital sheets seemed to hold out the promise of what I really wanted: a place of safety, a white oblivion. Oblivion, strictly speaking, was what I was after, but white hospital sheets were an approximation, I believed.

Actually, the reality of the hospital in London was rather different, though the sheets *were* white. The near-demented Sister Winniki (identical twin of Big Nurse) always ripped the crisp white sheets off me at too early an hour in the morning, in the name of mental health. 'Up, up, up, Mees Seemonds. Ve must not lie in bed, it vill make us depressed.' I was depressed and all I wanted were the right conditions for my depression, but we weren't allowed to be depressed in the bin. I spent eighteen months off and on during my early twenties in this and other hospitals in London, not getting what I was really after.

Sister Winniki was like a gust of wind. She breezed about her ward (or, as I thought of it, *my* ward) at remarkable speed, talking as she went in her South London inflected Estonian accent. 'How are ve today?' she would cry, but by the time you had thought up an answer she was gone. So, one patient was informed that today she had ECT, another one that if she didn't attend occupational therapy Sister would be compelled to inform the consultant, another that her medication had changed. Sister Winniki was on top of everything, though you felt that she was in control only for as long as she kept moving, clipping along on the backs of her heels, her black-stockinged legs scissoring, her bright-orange lipsticked mouth snapping out instruction and exhortation. A healthy ward of mental patients was, to her mind, a busy ward, but busyness is not what mental patients are best at, except, of course, those who are too good at it, so there was a permanent tension between Winniki's whirlwind and our languor. I had to battle against Sister Winniki to achieve even a modicum of oblivion – and since the whole point of oblivion is that it is total or not at all, I could never prevail.

When hospitalization failed, I transferred my fantasy to the idea of a monk's cell. A small, bare, white room with nothing to distract the eye from the emptiness, a strict routine of silence broken only by the regular rhythmic ritual of the liturgy, had all the advantages of hospital – spareness and passivity interspersed with meal and medication times – without the disadvantage of Sister Winniki. A fallacy, since doubtless there would be a Father Winniki to chivvy me into useful action. But there wasn't anywhere I could go with the fantasy, being both the wrong religion and the wrong sex, so I settled maturely, compromisingly, for making my almost blank bedroom and achieving at least my morning whiteout. It's

3

something, but not quite enough. Though I'm very good at getting what I want, the world is better at not letting me have more than a taste of it. Sister Winniki never quite goes away; eventually, I have to start the day and the empty white world fills up with colour.

Finally it came to me, effortlessly, as these things seem to come. Suddenly, there's a moment when a thought in your head makes itself known as if it's always been there, as if you've been thinking it forever. Sometimes I think I don't think at all, if thinking means some conscious process of the mind working out the nature and solution of a problem. I'm a little ashamed of this. I wish I thought properly, like proper people seem to think.

Still, the thought was there. Antarctica. And along with it a desire as commanding as any sexual compulsion that Antarctica was what I wanted, and that therefore I had to have it. I have not always longed to go to Antarctica, or even ever wanted to especially, but the thought was as powerful as if it had been a lifelong dream. Perhaps it's possible to have life-long dreams in retrospect.

Like a sexual compulsion, the Antarctic dream was inconvenient; it would involve doing something, taking time out of the regularity of life in the study, travelling – and I dislike the idea of travel. I reasoned with myself: throughout the history of the world very, very few people have been to Antarctica; there was no reason why I, just because I fancied it, should be among them. Statistics are designed to keep you safe. It wouldn't be an outrage if I didn't go to Antarctica, almost everybody didn't.

4

Nothing bad would happen if I reached the end of my life without having been there. But I was, none the less, outraged at the idea of not going. Irrationally but unmanageably outraged. This is very important to me, I replied to my reasoning self, but I was unable to explain why. As I said, much like a sexual compulsion.

The Arctic would have been easier, but I had no desire to head north. I wanted white and ice for as far as the eye could see, and I wanted it in the one place in the world that was uninhabited (never mind the penguins, seals and base camp personnel for the time being). I wanted a place where Sister Winniki couldn't exist. I wanted my white bedroom extended beyond reason. That was Antarctica, and only Antarctica.

It turned out not to be so easy to go to Antarctica. There isn't anywhere exactly to go. But like thoughts that pop into your head, classified advertisements make themselves known when you've got something on your mind. '*Antarctica – the cruise of a lifetime,*' it said. I sent off for the brochure. In the meantime, I called the British Antarctic Survey in Cambridge.

'How can I get to Antarctica?' I asked.

'Are you a scientist?'

'No, I'm a writer.'

It sounded feeble next to the echo of 'scientist'. The woman at the BAS clearly agreed.

'You can't go if you're not a scientist engaged in specific research.' Was she a relative of Sister Winniki?

'Why not?'

'Because the British Antarctic Survey is set up to protect the environment for serious scientific purposes.'

'What about serious writing purposes?'

She said she could arrange for me to interview people who had spent time on British Antarctic bases.

'Have you considered having a writer in residence?' I wondered.

To say she put the phone down wouldn't be quite true, but the conversation terminated.

I phoned around a little to people who might know, or people who might know people who might know. It became clear that the BAS was the key, and the only key, to getting on to the white continent and that my chances of persuading them were virtually nil. There were a very few places on their ships each year for the press, but when I phoned them back about it they told me those places were booked for two or three years ahead, mostly by BBC Television – a rather more respectable, and better resourced organization than I was ever going to appear. I could, if I wished, write in and apply for a place, but the likelihood of getting there seemed further away in time and probability than Antarctica was in space.

The possibility of a summer spent living in a camp on the boundless expanse of ice began to recede. The scientists, it seemed, had wrapped up an entire continent for their own and only their own purposes. No one could go without their say-so, because their objectives were pure, and being pure they were entrusted with the last pure place on earth. The rest of us are frivolous despoilers who need to be controlled. A poet or a

6

painter who wants to experience the emptiness and grandeur of the continent which, by treaty, belonged to no one and therefore I suppose to the poet and painter as much as anyone else, would not be able to go without massive financial resources of the kind poets and painters are not known to attract unless they're long dead. A pity. Antarctica is in the control of the scientists as Mecca is under the authority of the mullahs. Neither religion nor science has an unblemished record of spreading peace and harmony within their spheres of influence. A pity for poets; a nuisance for me.

I am not averse to disappointment. It has its own special pleasures. Disappointment is the hidden agenda within fantasy, a nugget for the *aficionado* who might trick up the bland negativity of the word by sliding alphabetically towards *disjunction* and *disparity*. If you could have what you dream about, if I could have Antarctica all white and solitary and boundless, there would finally be no excuse. Imagine, you are exactly where you want to be – and now what? Yes white, yes solitary, yes boundless, but will it, in its icy, empty, immense reality, do? In my head, it does fine, why seek out the final disappointment which the earlier, smaller disappointment only seeks to prevent? The point of desire is desire itself, the essential pleasure in expectation is expectation. The idea that gratification is a completion of the wish is fallacious. It is only our dim literal-mindedness that makes us believe that we should try to achieve what we wish for. Disappointment stands between the two like a guardian angel. The fissure between what I want and what I can have is my friend, my best friend in all likelihood, and I know it. Disappointment is a safety net, to be relished in a secret knowing way by the disappointed. Give thanks for the BAS and all the other preventers of fantasy come true.

The brochure arrived and I reset my daydreams.

Some realities you cannot get away from. I learned that, repeatedly, from the age of two at Queen's Ice Rink. An ice rink is as cruel a reminder of reality as any that has been devised. It is a surface artificially constructed to be as friction-free as you can get while having both feet on the ground – yet is enclosed on all sides by a wooden barrier. An ice rink is a promise made purely for the pleasure of creating disappointment. If you want to skate without stopping you have to go round and round the bounded ice; you can't go on and on, even though the surface permits a gathering of speed which can only be for the purpose of heading forwards without hindrance.

I'm not altogether ill at ease with boundaries. I was a city-bred child and boundaries are part of the nature of the city. Pavements stopped at kerbs and became roads, requiring a change of direction if I was on my tricycle, or a change of attention if I needed to cross to the next section of pavement. It was as obvious as breathing; the geography of my world didn't just go on and on. There were stopping places, turning points and breaks in the cityscape on any journey.

I lived on an island on an island. What I knew about the larger island was that if you went on in any direction there was sea at the edge of everywhere; the notion of a change of country without a watery division was astonishing to me. I first experienced it when I was very small: we went to Belgium and drove to Holland one day. I couldn't credit the unreality of it. It was the sea that said a country was a country, not an official checking passports at a border. And where were we, I wanted to know, when the car was halfway across the line dividing Belgium and Holland? 'It depends,' my father riddled, 'whether you're sitting in the front or back seat.' This was interesting, because I always sat in the front passenger seat next to my father when the three of us were in the car. My mother sat in the back. Always. Under the peculiar circumstances of the Belgium/Holland border, my father and I were a nation apart from my mother. I swivelled in my seat at the critical moment as we crossed into Belgium again that evening. 'You're still in Holland,' I told my mother, but even as I spoke she arrived back in Belgium with us.

The island within the greater island was a block of flats on the Tottenham Court Road. Paramount Court. Diagonally across the road, while I lived there, was a bomb site; at its northern end was Maples furniture shop, to the south the Eastman's dental school and the concrete cul-de-sac where my most enormous box of fireworks caught a spark and exploded. Behind the island of Paramount Court was Gower Street, the buildings of London University on one side, and University College Hospital on our side. To the west of the Paramount Court island, across Tottenham Court Road, were the nooks and crannies of Fitzrovia. Adjoining the northern side of the flats was an Odeon cinema – my cinema. In the well at the very centre of the block, surrounded by the back of the flats and the Odeon, was a broad alleyway leading from a black metal fire-escape, and past a dividing wall on the other side another alley led out from the back exit of the cinema. All this I remember as the fixed landscape of my early childhood.

Paramount Court is still there. I pass it in the car once or twice a week. If the lights are red on that corner, I can look up to the fifth floor and see the windows of the second flat we inhabited. I lived in Paramount Court with my mother and, when he was present, my father, from the time I was born until I was eleven, which is to say 1947 to 1958 or thereabouts. Until I was seven we lived in a two-roomed flat on the third floor, facing the well at the back, then we moved upstairs to the fifth floor to a three-roomed flat at the front where, from seven to eleven years old, I had a room of my own for the first time. Tottenham Court Road has changed. The traffic is one way now and there's much more of it; the cinema was pulled down years ago and the space remains unplugged, although it's been designated as the new hospital which will replace University College Hospital and the Middlesex. Then, of course, there were no electronics shops, there being nothing in the way of electronics in the fifties. The most important difference, to my imagination, is that the entrance to the flats now has a bank of entry buzzers. In my day, the front doors were open and visitors just went in and rode in the lift to the flat they wanted.

Those new entry phones, requiring one to have a precise destination and to state one's business at the threshold, may be the immediate cause of my recurrent dream that I am trying and failing to gain entry to the flats, specifically to get into my own flat. I press the buzzers and explain that I just want to look at where I used to live, but the intercom goes dead. Sometimes I scale the façade like a mountaineer and try to climb in through the windows, sometimes I simply fly, but I never manage to get inside the block to the corridors and stair-wells where I want so much to be. The windows are locked, or people open them only to push me away and down again to the pavement below.

The back alleyways of the flats and the cinema, and the skirt of pavement around the island of my flats, were my play-ground. I zipped round and round the block on tricycle, big red pedal-car, scooter and two-wheeler. I chalked the paving stones with hopscotch, and waylaid people who lived in the flats or were just walking along the street. It was my territory, my pave-ment. Prince Monolulu, who has since become a pub, lived in Fitzrovia and was a regular passer-by. He was immensely tall, ebony black, wore exotic flowing robes (exotic, that is, for those days) and always had brilliantly coloured cock feathers in his hair. He was a racing tipster and a professional character. When we met on my pavement, he'd yell out his catchphrase, 'I got a hoss. I got a hoss,' and we'd fall into each other's arms. He'd swing me around and tickle me, chuckling his pleasure at our meeting. I was delighted to be caught up in his iridescent, ebul-lient aura. Other regulars passed by who I knew, people going to

11

and from work or shopping, a couple of tramps doing their regular circuit, taxi drivers on their route. We'd greet each other and chat. They were part of my world.

Inside the flats, each of the corridors on the seven floors was long, narrow and L-shaped. At the far end of each long corridor were sparkling granite stairs which echoed feet and voices, though only occasionally, which made them exciting, because these were the back stairs, not often used. By the lifts, just before the corridor turned the corner of the L, were the front stairs, painted a dark green and a more public space for more sociable, less mystery-seeking moods. All these were play spaces, though the corridor that lay around the corner of the L was dangerous alien territory, like the forest at the edge of an isolated settlement, only to be entered if one was feeling exceptionally brave.

It never crossed my mind that my domain was limited in any way. The bareness of the narrow, cream-coloured empty corridors, the neutral carpet and the unadorned pavement was decorated and redesigned every day with whatever landscape I chose for it. It felt enormous, limitless, available for whatever purpose I wished to put it to, and filled with both familiarity and surprise. Even now I can't imagine any suburban or country childhood that would have provided me with so much. I spent a lot of time wandering, playing on my own, but there were other children in the block with whom I played in the spaces of the flats – Helen, Jonathan, Susan – whose doors I knocked on, with whom I would have tea sometimes, who occasionally would have tea with me in my flat. So, I still dream about getting back to roam in the corridors, to climb the fire-escape, to play the games and tell myself the stories I invented in my childspace.

Inside the enclosing walls of Paramount Court, I began life with parents who were cash rich. The profitable days of the black market were still enabling my father to bring plenty of money home, and the remains of the jewellery my mother had from her first husband was sold off to keep her feeling wealthy when the black market came to an end. For the first three or four years of my life, my mother's desperate need to display wealth was taken care of. Of all things in her life, I was the best medium for her display: she went abroad for my woollen vests (which I loathed for their scratchiness – 'they can't scratch, they're the best Belgium wool' – but they did, I swear, I can feel them now), dressed me in velvet-collared coats like the little Prince and Princess, and made sure I always wore white gloves and had immaculately ironed satin bows in my hair. Before I could read, my bookcase was full of every child's classic – fairy tales, nursery stories, wonderlands, neverlands – and several adult books that seemed as if they might be for children – *Jane Eyre*, *Gulliver's Travels*, *A Tale of Two Cities* – though the only book I recall my parents owning was *The Diary of a Nobody*. I went daily to skating and ballet lessons and had, in my first school, elocution as an extra. Both my parents were the children of working-class Jewish immigrants, they wanted material wealth for themselves and both material wealth and culture for their child. When the money dried up, my mother struggled heroically to maintain my appearance –

13

the white gloves were the last thing to go. But eventually, the money, the credit and my father all ran out for good and at the same time. By the time I was eleven, in the same block of flats, my mother and I lived in an empty shell, with everything, including my books, though not the white gloves, taken away by the bailiffs, and we were waiting to be evicted.

But for all my appreciation of boundaries, as a small child, the limits of the ice rink aggravated me. There's no reason, I suppose, why I shouldn't have wanted both things: the safely circumscribed but imaginatively enlargeable play territory at home, and an ice rink that ran on and on into infinity. Consistency is not a quality I've ever claimed very much to admire or possess.

As I recall, it was my mother who took me skating – every day, long before I was old enough to start school. You could skate before you could walk, she would say when I was older. There were white ankle-length boots, at first the smallest the shop at the rink could make, shiny silver skates and a white leather cover to protect the blades. Every few months there would have to be a new pair. I think I remember the push chair, and a snow suit I wore before progressing into a short skating skirt. I had a formal lesson every day for an hour and then was supposed to practise under the encouraging eye of my mother who sat behind the barrier just by the open entrance to the rink, wrapped in a heavy black cloth coat with a fur collar. It was a cold place for spectators, but mothers sat, warmly wrapped, sipping tea from the café, watching their children spin and speed around the ice. It's not a strong memory of her, just the sitting there and encouraging me to practise more.

The ice itself is more vivid, quite easily accessible to the memory banks in each of my senses. It's quite hard to recollect the experience of walking, even though I've just brought a cup of tea from my kitchen to my study. I have to concentrate to bring alive the sense of the ground under my feet, the rolling of each foot from heel to ball, the difference in quality of the change from wood flooring to carpeting. If I return to the kitchen, trying to be fully aware of what it feels like, I lose the essence of walking, which is that it is an unthinking process. Bring back the sensation and I lose the reality of it. Skating is different, even though I haven't done it since I was a small child. My feet have retained the memory of skating, but then it isn't a natural experience for feet to be constrained in an unbending boot from sole to ankle and raised on a quarter inch of steel blade so that they never actually touch the ground. Feet don't skate, but they experience skating. You sense the solidity of the ice through the blade in a way that is quite different from being on any other hard surface. Concrete doesn't feel as ungiving and absolute as ice. You slide over its surface, but there is no engaging with it, no sense, as you get even with concrete, certainly with rock and paving stones, of surface texture, of tiny undulations, of there being earth beneath. Rink ice is a solid block, whose depth you sense as you slick across its surface, as a swimmer senses the fathoms beneath them buoying them up. But the sea moves, engages with the body of the swimmer, while the ice is enigmatic, separate from the skater.

15

And yet, to skate is magical, as you find yourself coasting free and frictionless. The clear distinction between yourself and the ice you are on strengthens the sensation of your own body and its capacity both for control and for letting appropriate things happen. And for all the perception of physical mastery, skating is still strange and dreamlike. Dreams of flying are the nearest you get to the feeling of being on the ice.

The cold of the ice wafts up at you, rising like heat from a radiator until it hits your unprotected face. A dry cold sensation on your cheeks is odd because you are indoors and this feels like weather. My feet also remember the awkwardness of walking on the rubber matting to get on to the rink. Sitting on the chair next to my mother with my boot on her lap, first one pushed firmly on, then the other, the jerking taut of the laces at each eyelet – the tightness of the laces around the ankle, keeping it rigid was vital – then the winding of the laces and the final double bow. I couldn't do it myself at first. Then, with my skate guards still on, I'd walk across the matting to the gap in the barrier, all clumpy and wobbly, because the matting was criss-crossed with small square holes through which the back of the blade got snagged sometimes. No one gave lessons in walking on the ordinary ground in ice skates, but the ungainliness was a pleasure for the distinction it made as I stood on the edge of the rink, took off the guards and then took a first step on to the ice. All the clumsiness disappeared. Suddenly, I was perfectly equipped, steel blade matching glossy ice, and I'd slide proficiently and casually along the few feet to hand the guards to my mother over the barrier, her on one side, me in another medium altogether. I'd push away the barrier with my hand and cruise to the other end of the rink, the skates making a sound of knives being sharpened. I was like a duck shaking off the memory of land as it slides and glides into its intended element.

Every hour the skating stopped and a machine was pushed up and down the ice, like a lawn mower, to smooth it. The top layer gathered in the parabolic collector in front of the machine, a growing heap of snow-like, frost-like debris, and was pushed ahead, as the machine scraped away the surface, scored by the dozens of skates in the past hour, dragging sideways across the ice to come to a halt, or turning sharply in their tracks, or pitting the surface by digging the serrated front end of the blade into it to get a good speedy push-off. It was all taken away in minutes and underneath was pure, untouched surface again, gleaming milky-white, virgin, immaculate ice. For fifteen minutes after this the rink was only for serious skating; people practising what they had learned during a lesson, and rehearsing dance routines to the music coming from loudspeakers. In the middle, figures were skated, and I would go on with a handful of others and practise making 2s, 3s, 4s, all the single digits, appear in the silky new ice. This was another kind of skating, not going anywhere, rather meditative, concentrating on the ice at your feet to assess the quality of the marks that were appearing under your blade. I don't remember the rights and wrongs of it but the edges of the blade were critical: which edge – inside or outside – you used, skating backwards, to make the top curve in the 2, how you turned and skated forward on the inside (or the outside) edge to make the tail. You engraved the number on the ice over and over again to make it balanced, with the right degree of curve and the right length of tail. At the time, I railed against this formal skating. I wanted to speed along, twisting sharply to skate backwards, then reversing, skate forwards, to make little jumps scissoring my legs, and then dig in the point of my blade and increase the speed still more as I landed. These figures were the building blocks of such free and flashy skating, I was told. They would teach me balance and control on the ice. The figure 2 had me turning and leaning so that I could eventually skate in just the way I wanted, but I had to work at it to get the technique right. I didn't want to get the technique right, I could pretty much do what I wanted to do without perfect technique, and I had a natural sense of balance. It was boring making 2 appear over and over again on the surface of the ice when I could have been flying free.

Now, I like the idea of that slow, concentrated, meticulous and pointless activity. Eyes down watching the blade and glancing behind to check on the quality of the mark you have made, seeing it not quite correct, not bulbous enough, or unevenly rounded, finding the tail too elongated, not sharply enough defined, and beginning again to make it better, eventually to make it right. It's that I imagine myself doing now, not the fancy twirls, spins or that wonderful arcing movement as you lie back on the air and spread your feet, heels pointing towards each other, legs wide, to glide a lazy, backward centrifugal semi-circle. I watch the champions making gorgeous use of their

18

techniques, but find myself daydreaming about being on a rink involved in the arcane intricacies of making an eventually perfect 3 appear on the glazed, pristine surface of the ice.

My mother didn't find my endlessly practising figures on the ice pointless; she was willing to sit day after day in the chilly seat beside the barrier. She never once thought of getting on the ice herself. The figures were for her, as for my skating teacher, a means to an end. They would make me the new Sonja Henie, the skating champion turned skating movie star. I would be the youngest champion ice skater ever, and she would be the mother of the champion. It would mean fame, money, travel and a good marriage, and she would accompany me on the route to all these good things. My mother dreamed of making me into an ice princess, but something went wrong. After a while I refused to practise, and life, in any case, got in the way. What she got, to her bitter disappointment, though I think the irony might have been lost on her, was an ice maiden of another kind altogether.

Whenever, in the past thirty years, people have asked, as they do in the regular way of introductory conversations, about my parents, my answer has been that my father died in 1966 and that I haven't seen or heard from my mother since the same date. Often, incongruously to my mind, they would subsequently ask me if she is still alive. 'I don't know,' I would reply, because I didn't.

'But don't you want to know?'

'No.'

'You must,' some soul brother or sister of Sister Winniki will insist.

There seems to be no limit to the reach and power of popular psychology. Everyone now knows that mothers are an essential item of equipment in any psyche, and that though relations with mothers may be difficult or even dreadful, attachment to them is mandatory. They also know, as a corollary, that a denial of attachment is a failure to confront the reality of mother-attachment.

'You must find it very disturbing.'

'No, I find it delightful.'

However, I, being no less of my time than anyone else, am not immune to the power of popular psychology, for all my doubts and irritations with it. I knew what I felt about my mother's absence, but suspected that what I felt must be an avoidance of the real feelings everyone else supposed I naturally would have. Bad feelings, sad feelings, guilt feelings. Those kind of feelings. From time to time, in the cause of self-knowledge, I would excavate, try to dig down below my contentment with the situation, but beyond the strong wish for the situation and therefore my contentment to continue, I could find no underlying seismic fault waiting to open up. Of course, psychoanalytic theory has a ready answer to this – how could I investigate my own unconscious? No one, it claims, apart from Freud, could do it successfully. True enough, if you accept the idea of a lurking unconscious dedicated to keeping information from our waking, and indeed sleeping, selves. How can I possibly know what I don't know I know? There's no argument against this one. Still, there were a few things I did know about myself which might equally have been concealed from me by me, and some of those things gave me pain and difficulty. Perhaps the continuing enigma of my absent mother shielded me from something worse, uncopable with. Indeed it did, it shielded me from her if she happened still to be alive. But if that was the case, then shouldn't I have been grateful to my unconscious for the protection it provided? Surely, it is neurotic to seek pain, where ordinary unhappiness is available? Psychoanalysis has inclined us to think of the unconscious as our enemy, to be overcome, but perhaps it's more of a partner in survival. What, apart from Puritanism, even perhaps sadism, makes anguished awareness of the kind our unconscious seeks to prevent, so very desirable? That fully analysed person, the one whose unconscious is laid bare, who is in command of their psyche: what dreams do they have, what games can they play, and who can they talk to on equal terms, in a world where the vast majority of us are rubbing along leading an altogether murkier sort of inner life? Defensive, all of this, of course. Even so. I gave up searching for anguish and settled for naive tranquillity. What I didn't know didn't seem to hurt me.

For the most part, quantum theory has been of little practical use in my life. When shopping in Sainsbury's, trying to get out of bed in the morning, working out my VAT, or wondering what to wear, quantum theory is hardly any help. In one area, however, it has had a remarkable relevance.

With all due acknowledgement to Erwin Schrödinger,* let us do a thought experiment. Imagine a box, inside which is a flask of hydrocyanic acid, some radioactive material, a Geiger counter – and my mother. The apparatus is wired up so that if the radioactive material decays, the Geiger counter will be triggered and will set off a device to shatter the flask and thereby kill my mother. We set the experiment up, shut the lid of the box, and wait until there is a precise fifty-fifty chance that the radioactive decay has occurred. What is the state of my mother *before* we open the lid to look?

Common sense says that my mother is either alive or dead, but according to quantum theory, events such as the radio-active decay of an atom and therefore its consequences become real only when they are observed. The case is not decided until someone opens the lid and looks. The condition of the radioactive material in the closed box is known as a *superposi-tion of states*, an inextricable mixture of the decayed and not-decayed possibilities. Once the box is open and we look inside it, one of the options becomes reality, the other disap-pears. But before we look, everything in the box, including my mother, exists in a superposition of states, so my mother is, in quantum theory terms, both dead and alive at the same time for as long as the box is closed.

*And John Gribben's explanation in *In Search of the Edge of Time* which I paraphrase here.

Since I came across this thought experiment, it has been my view that whatever psychoanalytic theory might have to say about the matter of my mother, it would first have to do battle with, and best Schrödinger, before it could fully win me over. The choice on offer is the assumption that for thirty years I repressed curiosity about my mother's existence because thoughts of her were intolerable, or that, all unknown to me, I was contentedly, not to say harmoniously, living out a recognized phenomenon of the known physical universe. We could go a step further, and say that until the lid of a second psychoanalytic versus quantum box is opened, the choice between the two theories remains in a superposition of states.

It would certainly have opened this latter box just a little and moved the decision slightly in the direction of the shrinks had my desire to get to the great white continent come after the box containing my mother had been opened and her positional state been clarified once and for all. But, in fact, the mother box was still closed, and there was only the merest suggestion that it could ever be opened. Still, I acknowledge that the faint threat existed, and leave the lid on the second box at least ajar in the name of fairness.

I last saw my mother on 22 April 1966. You may find my certainty of the date significant, but I remember it because I know the last time I saw her was two days after my father died. The date in my memory is the date of his death.

When I was fourteen, I was admitted, after an overdose, to the mental hospital in Hove where I stayed for four and a half months, stuck, because the psychiatrist in charge wouldn't let me live with either of my parents. My father was in Banbury, my mother in Hove. The mother of a schoolfriend heard about me and offered me a home in her house in London which I, the psychiatrist and both my parents gratefully accepted. When my father died in 1966 I was still living in her house, aged eighteen, and two months away from taking my A-levels.

Two days after my father died, my mother came through the front door and handed me an umbrella. A gift. For April showers and stormy weather. It wasn't any ordinary umbrella, it was pale, powder-blue and shaped like a pagoda, its spire rising to a delicate point, and all around the base was a scalloped frill made of a matching powder-blue, nylon chiffon-like material. Look for the chiffon lining – blue skies, nothing but blue skies – on the sunny side of the street – every time it rains it rains pennies from heaven – come rain or come shine.

I hadn't been in contact with my father for over a year and, apart from a nasty moment over my hospital bed in Hove, my mother hadn't seen him for a lot longer than that. He had died of a heart attack, his second in a few months. After the first attack, Pam, the woman he was living with, had written to my mother asking her to let me know. She hadn't.

My mother sat down to lunch. She was almost feverishly elated. *She was pleased he was dead. It served him right for being*

24

the bastard he was. And she wasn't a hypocrite. She'd always said, hadn't she always said – she had always said – that if she saw him lying dead in the gutter she'd kick him out of the way and walk by. And that's what she would do if she saw him now lying in his coffin. She'd spit on him right as he lay there. And laugh. But, as a matter of fact, she didn't think he was really dead, anyway. She thought he was just pretending to be dead, the lying scheming louse that he was, so that he wouldn't have to pay her the £5 a month alimony. She thought . . .

The woman I was living with was present and at this point, thinking I needed something more than a blue umbrella, reminded me about an A-level class I had to get to. I'd better hurry, she said, or I'd miss it. I hurried so much getting out of the house to the non-existent class that I forgot to take any money with me, so I wandered down to Camden High Street and took sanctuary in the library, prepared to give it a couple of hours before my mother ran out of steam and went on her way. The library had a large plate-glass window, and my mother, instead of turning left to the nearest tube and bus stop when she got to the High Street, inexplicably turned right and walked right past the library window. Not actually past. She was already screaming when she pushed through the doors. I sat in silence while she shrieked and wept, noisily enumerating my faults, not the least of which was being just like him: a liar, deceitful, treacherous, heartless. All true, actually, in this context. It provided some dramatic entertainment for the tramps keeping warm, a couple of genuine students and the mothers and children choosing their books for the week, to whom she turned to witness the tragedy of a woman with an unnatural daughter. Then she departed, her aria over, leaving the library in a silence it rarely achieved in the normal course of the day. I watched her disappear past the window in the direction of Camden Town underground, and then, I supposed, back to Hove, after her day out in London. I never saw her again.

My father's death was an extraordinary event, but my mother's dramatics were not, though she had outdone herself being, I had to acknowledge, probably distraught about my father. Usually, after a scene like this, there would be a silence and then she would get in touch again. I wasn't surprised not to hear from her for a while.

My mother's silence continued, and I didn't do anything about it. I didn't want to speak to her, and the fact that she didn't want to speak to me was a relief, putting off the next unpleasantness. The silence elongated into months, then years and then decades. I dumped school just before the exams, moved into a bedsit, sank into depression and began my second period of hospitalization. After eighteen months I had a choice – spend the rest of my life doing the rounds of London bins, or practise real life. I went to teacher training college, became a teacher in a comprehensive school in Hackney, married, changed my name and had my daughter when I was thirty, wrote and published my first novel at thirty-five, wrote more novels. From time to time I'd think about the possibility that my mother would get in touch with me, and a slight panic would flutter through me. I never thought of getting in touch with her. There were periods when asking for trouble was something to which I seemed to be dedicating my life, but even at my worst I knew better than to ask for that kind of trouble – it was too familiar, too distressing. It came to seem like an act of kindness eventually. The one truly generous act of my mother's that I could really put my finger on: her leaving me alone. I knew, of course, that in her mind she was disowning me, sloughing off a daughter whose lack of gratitude was monstrous, though in this case I *was* grateful. Even so, it wasn't like my mother to leave anyone alone for very long. It was entirely out of character. She had no friends or family, none that she spoke to, anyway. I was all she had left to keep her disappointed. But I suspected she had a man friend. There was a man who came to see me with her when I was in the hospital in Hove. He walked into my ward, a small, white-bearded, plump man – quite nice-looking, I thought – and slapped me hard around the face, though it was more surprise than violence that made me lose my balance and fall on to the bed. 'That's for what you have done to your mother,' he said, taking my mother by the arm and marching out of the room. I'd never seen him before, or since, but perhaps he was still around, giving her encouragement, and to him too I was grateful.

After years of silence I concluded that either she had found someone more satisfactory than me to live her life around, or perhaps she was dead. Suicide was a possibility, if the past was anything to go by, but the chances of her committing suicide, or trying to, and not making absolutely sure I knew about it, seemed remote. My daughter, Chloe, was growing up and began asking after her other granny, the one she never had tea with on Sundays. I explained the situation in stages. She had, on her father's side, a voluminous set of relations: uncles, aunts, cousins, great-uncles, grandfather and grandmother. I really didn't know about my mother and didn't think Chloe's, but especially my own, life would be improved by finding out. I'd long ago lost and forgotten her address. She had been living in Hove in 1966, but she could be anywhere now. Intrigued by this missing granny, and rather moved that she might be walking around the world all unaware that she had been blessed with a granddaughter, Chloe suggested when she was about twelve that we visit Brighton. 'We might see her on the street,' she said.

I felt I hadn't quite conveyed the nature of my mother, due to some conventional sense that small children ought to hear more regular family tales, so I enlarged a little on the character of her missing granny, and how she was unlikely to be the sweet little old lady she had in mind. This seemed to quell her curiosity. One day, however, we did go to Brighton. I had to do a reading there, and must have been feeling a little emotionally reckless when I agreed to do it. Chloe came along to throw pebbles in the sea and to have a posh tea at the Grand.

'So listen, kid,' I told her on the train, 'if you see a wild, screaming old woman coming down the street, probably with a kitchen knife in her hand, yelling at me, run like hell. You'll catch up with me if you really make the effort.' She enjoyed the joke, but I spent the day keeping well away from Hove, trying to conceal my jitters, glancing over my shoulder and casing every shop and café before we went in for the kind of old lady who might turn into my mother.

In order to find out if my mother was alive or dead, I would have had to open the box. Miraculously, my mother had climbed into the box and closed the lid herself. If I had lifted the lid, I would have discovered that one option was reality and the other disappeared. I had no desire for the option of her still being alive to become real. It was fine by me if she was alive, but I didn't want what would result from it. Some realities you *can* get away from. The other possible reality, that she was dead, would have maintained the *status quo*, but the risk of finding the wrong reality just to satisfy a curiosity – which I didn't seem to have – was too great.

But what about attachment? How could this primary maternal connection have passed me by? Clearly, I was either fatally emotionally damaged goods, or I was in possession of the healthiest psyche since psychoanalytic annals began. There was another possibility: that I was plain bad, as heartless and unfeeling as my mother always supposed me to be. What gave this latter option the edge was that I was able to countenance it quite calmly. If the idea of being bad and unfeeling didn't make me feel bad, bad was probably just what I was. If anywhere, this badness was where my attachment to my mother existed. It was an area of agreement, with different implications for each of us, that we held separately but in common. When Sister Winniki's spiritual friends and relations asked me if I wasn't disturbed by the riddle of my mother's absence, they meant didn't I feel guilty about not knowing or caring. And I didn't. Which made me all three of the above: emotionally damaged, healthy as a horse, and bad. But guilt-free. And perhaps this was a gift freely, albeit unwittingly, given to me by my mother. If I could live with the imponderable condition of my mother in her closed box, I seemed also able to live with my own imponderable state. I'm not dismayed by contradiction. I get depressed from time to time. I don't like it, but I'm not surprised or baffled by it. Neither is my GP. 'You've never dealt with your deprivation and despair,' he says, being a believer in psychological heal- ing. But I do, in my way. I deal with it all the time, and quite well.

Chloe was halfway through her A-level course when she asked me one day how you find out if someone is dead. I was eva- sive, as far as I knew there was only one person whose life or death status was in doubt.

'You could try asking them. If they don't answer, reckon they're dead.'

But let's say my liberalism and belief in the benefits of edu- cation got the better of me.

'Find out if there's a death certificate.'

Funny how easy and obvious it was, and what a nonsense it made of 'I don't know if my mother is alive or dead'.

'How?'

'They used to keep birth, marriage and death certificates in Somerset House, but they moved them.'

Suddenly, and with all the convenience my unconscious could muster, I couldn't remember where they moved them to.

'Don't do it.' More of a plea than a command.

'I'll just find out if she's dead, that's all.'

'It won't prove anything if there isn't a death certificate. She could have remarried and died under another name.'

'But if there's a death certificate we'll know. And if there isn't one, I can check the marriage certificates and find out if she changed her name.'

This was burgeoning into a full-blown research project. My daughter the gumshoe was being born.

'So if there isn't a new marriage certificate and there isn't a death certificate?'

'Then we'll know she's alive.'

'Exactly.'

'That's all. We'll just know.'

It's not often that I notice the difference thirty years makes in people's understanding of the world. Chloe's belief that she would find out that her mysteriously absent grandmother was alive, and do nothing about it was, at that moment, genuine. Here was evidence that experience really does give you a little more information about the way folks are.

'I forbid you to do it.'

'You can't.'

'I know.'

I made a hurried set of rules, knowing it was as idle as Chloe's belief that finding no death certificate would be the end of it.

'If you want to do it, you have to do it yourself. I don't want to know about it. You'll have to pay for any costs yourself, I'm not going to finance it.'

She agreed, but was I sure I didn't want to know anything? She knew, she said, I was interested, *really*. Popular psychology and Sister Winniki stalked my house. She had an idea; if there was a death certificate she'd tell me, if there wasn't she wouldn't say a word.

I pointed out the fatal flaw in this plan, but I knew it was to no avail. I really hadn't considered the possibility that while the existence of Schrödinger's box meant blissful ignorance for me, it also meant that the lid could be lifted by someone else. My only hope was that A-level essays and a lively social life would take precedence over dull research in St Catherine's House.

No one had mentioned this when I was pregnant. They tell you things that you hardly take in at the time: about how much sleep you will be deprived of, how much worry you are about to incur, how your life will never be quite the same again. You nod to all this, and somehow manage to believe that none of these things will be true for you, until twelve hours after your child is born. But what they don't tell you is that one day they will get to be eighteen, and intellectually inquisitive and autonomous, and they'll go digging around in things that have remained satisfactorily enigmatic for most of your life. They don't tell you that they will consider their business what has been only your business. They don't tell you that after the education you so approve of, they will be equipped to find out what you have been evading for thirty contented years. They don't tell you that their need to test their powers will override the arrangements you have made with your psyche to keep things manageable. Or perhaps they do, and I wasn't listening.

I had a full year's grace. Essay-writing, clubbing and exam tension kept genealogical curiosity at bay, but in the autumn of 1995, when the school-leaving celebrations were finally over, exam results were through, and not long after I had booked my cabin on the Antarctic cruise for late November, the subject came up again.

'Where's St Catherine's House?'

It seemed she had managed to do a little preliminary research even in the midst of exam fever.

'Look it up,' I said, reinforcing my passive resistance.

'Mother,' she calls me mother when she feels she needs to be firm with me. 'You know you'll be pleased to find out what's happened to her.'

'Daughter, you are wrong.'

'But you are curious. Whatever you say.'

'If it makes it any easier for you to do it with the knowledge that I really do want to know, then I want you to know that I really, sincerely, profoundly do *not* want to know what happened to my mother.'

33

She smiled one of those patronizing smiles therapists and one's children smile, made for the telephone directory and then headed out the door.

'Off to St Catherine's House. See you later.'

An hour or so later, there was a phone call.

'What was her maiden name, how do you spell Rene, and where was she born?'

'I told you I'm not helping.'

'No, listen, I'll just get the birth certificate and marriage certificate to your dad. There's nothing wrong with that, is there? Anyway, I haven't got enough money to get a death certificate as well, even if there is one, and I can't do a search for it without knowing her maiden name and date of birth. Then they can do a search to find out if she remarried, in case she died under another name.'

'I hate this. Rayner. She wasn't born Rene. It was Rachel, I think. I'm not sure. I don't know when she was born, I think she was in her late thirties when she had me in 1947. She'd have been born in the East End.'

'Brilliant. The books are in periods of five years. That should do it.'

Though my mind said no, good citizenship told me she had as much right to that information as I did. It wasn't that I was already getting interested in this, just a case of not wanting to hamper an admirable exercise in basic research. Nothing more. Really.

The two certificates arrived in the post some days later. Chloe waved them at me over the kitchen table. I shook my head.

'Don't want to see. I know she was born and I know she was married.'

'But what about this "formerly Sherotsky"?'

'Show me.'

I'd forgotten she'd been married when she met my father. A man named Sherrick, it came back to me, in the rag trade. 'I should have stayed married to him,' I remembered. Sherrick, it seemed, had changed his name, as my father had, to seem less foreign, less Jewish. The marriage certificate *was* interesting. Rachel Sherotsky, otherwise Sherrick, formerly Rayner, whose condition was described as 'formerly the wife of Jack Sherotsky, otherwise Sherrick from whom she obtained a divorce,' had married James Simmonds, name changed by deed poll, whose condition was 'formerly the divorced husband of Melissa Simmonds, formerly Rosen, spinster'. James Simmonds' father's name was Samuel Zimmerman, a refreshment caterer having begun a new life in a new country and opened a café in Petticoat Lane. Rachel Simmonds' father was Morris Rayner, apparently of independent means. Rachel and James both gave their residence at the time of marriage as 38 Paramount Court, and his rank or profession as General Agent. There was just a line through the profession column for Rachel. He was thirty-five and she was thirty-six when they married on Christmas Eve, 1946.

A little finger counting made her two months pregnant with me on the happy occasion.

'Ooops,' said Chloe.

'Ooops,' said I.

All those otherwises and formerlies; all those names, hers and his, changed and disposed of. No Rene in sight. And, at last, my two grandfathers had names, though not their wives: Samuel and Morris.

My mother's birth certificate finally brought one grand-mother into view: Esther Rayner, formerly Shinars. And Morris's occupation turned out to be a hairdresser (Master). Rachel, girl, was born on 24 October 1910 at 376 Commercial Road in the district of Mile End Old Town. These were the documentary facts about my mother. Still, none of it applied to the adult woman who had vanished from my life, or from whose life I had vanished in 1966. None of it opened the box.

'Interesting, isn't it?' Chloe said, breaking the silence.

It was a while before Chloe returned to St Catherine's House, so it wasn't until one day in early October, about six weeks before I was due to go to Antarctica, that I got a call from her. She had said she was going out, but she hadn't mentioned where.

'Mum, there's a Rachel Simmonds in the book who died in hospital in 1988.' She sounded cautious. 'What do you think?'

'I think it sounds as if it could be her.'

'Should I order a copy of the death certificate? It could be someone else. It's not Rene and it's not Hove.'

'Go on, order it,' I said. 'I'll pay.'

The flight between London and Buenos Aires felt endless, at first helped and then hampered by the miniature animated plane on the visual display, which showed where we were presently on the map and how far we had yet to go. At first it was encouraging to watch the image of ourselves flying south, past the borders of the UK and across the Channel. The problem started around southern Spain when it became clear how little of the globe we had traversed, as Africa and the Atlantic Sea came into view. It was impossible not to look at the display; to let things just take their course, though when I have ever just let things take their course, I can't recollect. By the time we had passed North Africa, turned westish, and were travelling south towards and down the coast of South America, it had become a kind of torture. I'd shut my eyes, determined not to look for a decent length of time, but then had to peek, just to check that the little aeroplane icon had moved a bit. It hadn't, or seemed not to. The display and my peeks were too continuous to give any real sense of progress and it was disconcerting to read that we were travelling at over 500 miles an hour while appearing to get nowhere. I idled the time away, up in the air between there and there; here but nowhere, not even a border check to give me the feeling that I was passing through several heres on the way to there. I have it in my head that I like being suspended in travel from one place to another, but it doesn't seem to be the case. The urge to get somewhere, even if it's only the next stage on the journey is quite strong. It crossed my mind that this was true of writing, too. I like the *idea* of being midway through a book, of being in the midst of work, but the reality is that I'm constantly checking the word count and doing sums to see how soon I will finish the thing. Once it's finished, of course, it's bereft-time, and the sinking feeling that I was only on my way to the next book after all. Each book a way-station, a borderland to be crossed to the following book. Where's the terminus? At least on the plane I knew the route: from Heathrow to Buenos Aires, from Buenos Aires to Ushuaia in Patagonia, with a change of plane at Rio Gallegos, and then the ship to the Antarctic Peninsula. I suppose the book route ends up in the great whiteout, too. Best not think about that.

We did eventually get to São Paolo, though it was a bit of a surprise since we weren't supposed to. We descended for an unscheduled stop of an hour on the airport runway because, the pilot told us, we had run short – how short? – of fuel due to the unprecedented headwinds we had encountered. I was delighted that he hadn't mentioned these unprecedented headwinds earlier; I wouldn't say I was a nervous flyer so much as a very brave flyer under the most regular circumstances. By that I mean that once the equipment (so they called it on the itinerary) I'm in is racing at an alarming speed along the runway, I know that I am going to die and become suffused with the kind of deep calm only the profoundly hysterical can experience. Any kind of extraordinary circumstances would have snapped my fatalistic thread.

Still, it seemed careless on the part of the petrol pump attendants at Heathrow not to have taken headwinds, even of the extraordinary kind, into account when preparing for a thirteen-hour flight. There is a kind of logic, it turned out later. The birding British Airways purser who was on the cruise explained to me that there is a critical quantity of fuel for a plane. Sufficient to get you where you are going is good, but too much fuel (in our case, enough) causes, on account of the extra weight, extra fuel to be used. So more is less in the world of aviation as it sometimes is in life. Luckily, they were in at São Paolo airport and had some spare petrol, so apart from the despair of having to spend another hour on an already long flight, no harm was done.

I can and often have spent thirteen or fourteen hours at home whiling away the time reading, watching videos, brooding, staring, but somehow the same activities on a plane do not pass the time amiably. There's all the sitting down, of course, that might make an intolerable difference for some, but I'm no kind of active person. My real problem was the feeling that the dire Hollywood movie I'd been trapped into watching as the only viable alternative to the sodding aeroplane icon, and the face of Brad Pitt, might be the last things I saw in this life. A more depressing thought I couldn't imagine. If they played Beethoven's Late Quartets or Dinah Washington singing

Jerome Kern, and flashed up Rembrandt self-portraits, or photos of Robert Mitchum in his moody prime, I believe I'd be an altogether more contented traveller.

Finally we arrived to spend the night in Buenos Aires before another four- or five-hour flight to Ushuaia early next morning. It was the first chance to identify and meet the other people from the UK who were to be on the cruise. There were just six of us who gathered in a small huddle amid the American majority as we were greeted and given instructions on how to find places to eat. They were a fearfully hardy-looking lot, the British contingent, myself excluded. Aside from the BA purser, who was wearing a neat dark suit and tie, their chosen travelling gear was trekking boots, plus fours and shooting sticks, though in the torpid, gasoline-drenched heat of midsummer Buenos Aires, I reckoned my T-shirt and baggy cotton trousers had the edge. The Brits, apart from one couple, were 'birders' – *twitchers* was a term they twittered crossly at – a new breed of enthusiasts to me, though doubt-less I would find out more over the next three weeks.

Apart from nipping out between naps to have supper with Mona, a very elderly 'birder' from Edinburgh who designated me her travelling meal companion, I slept through my Buenos Aires hours. We were to have a full day and night in Buenos Aires on our return, and I was feeling too ragged to even think about joining the other Brits, who marched off in a body to visit a notable bird sanctuary on the outskirts of the city, when the sanctuary of a bed was just an elevator ride away. It's a fact that though I've often been to Paris, I've still only seen the

Eiffel Tower from a distance. I wondered what it is like to be avid for experience, but not for long, as I sank blissfully and incuriously into sleep.

Everyone asked Mona how old she was and on each upstart American who dared to voice such a query she fixed a slightly shrunken eye and said 'Och, what a question!' in high, disdainful Edinburgh tones. I had to suppose Mona concealed her age not from vanity, since her tiny, bent body, sparse wispy hair, and plain, washed, wrinkled face couldn't be mistaken for anything other than decidedly elderly, but that her reticence came from gentility and a pre-Generation X sense that personal questions are not good form. She told me over dinner that I would see how she straightened up in the dry air of the Antarctic Circle. She believed it to be the damp that made her back bend so that her natural glance was floorward. Her appetite was astonishing and I watched her pack away a steak the size of her plate and a bowlful of chips plus the remains of mine. When the dessert menu arrived she became coy. 'Oooh, no I couldn't. I've eaten so much. A little chocolate ice-cream, perhaps. I love ice-cream.' The waiter and I encouraged her, and giggling a little at her wickedness, she polished off the mountainous portion as if the film had been speeded up. It wasn't clear where all this substance could have gone in the tiny curved space that constituted Mona.

Once she began to talk, she didn't stop. Providing the proprieties were observed, she chattered with alarming enthusiasm about whatever was on her mind, and during the two meals we shared in Buenos Aires and the following day in

Ushuaia, she didn't have time to ask me a single question about myself. Birds were mostly what was on her mind. I learned a good deal about bird-watching, though very little about birds. I discovered that it is the watching, or rather the capturing through binoculars of a bird item, rather than the creature itself that is the main passion of the bird-watching fraternity on the trip. Mona, who was left well-provided for by her husband Ted, and who had learned to keep a canny eye herself on her stocks, was a world-traveller. In the past year or so she had visited Cuba, Hispaniola, Bhutan and Fiji in search of birds to add to her list. Next year, Australia and Bolivia and Surinam were blocked in. 'I used to collect numbers, but now I collect families,' she said mysteriously. 'This isn't a particularly interesting trip for me. You see, there aren't many different species of birds in Antarctica and they aren't on my list, but there is one bird from a particular family that you only find in Patagonia. That's what I'm after.'

Mona also collected thimbles and had a valuable stamp collection, giving the lie to my assumption that thing-collection is a male activity. It was Ted, however, who initiated her into the world of aggregation. 'He taught me so much.' Not just stamp- and bird-collecting, but fell-walking and golf. They had no children in their long and apparently contented marriage, but Ted was one of nature's enthusiasts. 'If I hadn't taken an interest, what would have happened to me? I'd have been left behind.' And when she was left behind, at last, she had those interests, like a good investment, to keep her active. The only cloud in their marriage was Ted's refusal to countenance the reality of death, which made his long, final illness all the more painful for both of them. 'It was never mentioned. He couldn't bear to talk about it, not even when he was well. I think he knew how ill he was at the end, though. One day I found a letter from the insurance company with details of his policy on the side-board. Ted knew I would dust there.' It was as near as he could get to saying goodbye.

The following morning, on the flight to Ushuaia, I extended my acquaintance of my fellow cruisers. Big Jim sat next to me on the plane, a man so vast that he spilled over his seat and shared half of mine. When the steward arrived with an extension for his seat belt, his fatness was unignorable. But in all likelihood, Big Jim would always indicate that he was aware of his size almost as soon as he introduced himself, just to clear the air. It wasn't quite 'Hello, I'm Jim and I am a very fat person' but close. 'Are you warm enough?' he asked me, indicating the air spouts above us. 'I'm always warm enough, I carry my own insulation around with me.' I smiled, but when the snack came and we had to lower the tables, Big Jim's rested at a precipitous angle on the mountain plateau of his belly so that his food tray slid precariously down to the back of the seat in front of him. He could only eat by putting the table back up and perching the tray on top of his stomach which started only inches from the lowest of his chins. His shame and embarrassment were palpable and I sat beside him trying to make myself seem larger.

Big Jim was a general practitioner in some desert town near Palm Springs, which made his reading a book called *Managing*

Hypertension seem more professional than privately desperate. He didn't read for long. I learned that he lives with six cats and a garage full of the Hollywood videos he collects. 'I've never been a small person,' he said apropos of nothing except what is continually on his mind, 'but 1989 I got thyroid cancer and my wife was killed in a car crash. Not a real good year. After the treatment I just blew up and I've been this size ever since.' In his surgery he has a low stool which he sits on when dealing with children. 'I'm so big, I frighten them unless I'm down at their level.' He's a regular solo traveller now. Lately he'd been to Ethiopia, Zimbabwe, Egypt and South Africa, while a woman in the town drops in to look after his cats. Just sitting in an aeroplane seat required special attention, and getting off the plane down the narrow aisle looked positively dangerous, not least for the queue waiting behind him who would never disembark if he got stuck in the narrow doorway. I couldn't imagine what difficulties his Third World, exotic travel must involve.

At Rio Gallegos we had to change to a smaller plane for the forty-five minute journey across the Beagle Channel to Tierra del Fuego's capital city: Ushuaia. I worried about Big Jim. A *smaller* plane. While we were waiting in the airport to board I met Less Big Jim, merely beer-gutted and ordinarily over-weight, an eager-faced greying US citizen with a touch of the shy but not so simple Ernest Borgnine about him. He told me he was from Saratoga Springs in upstate New York. I spent Christmas a few years back near there, I told him, in the home town of the man I lived with at the time; Ballston Spa, he'd probably heard of it. In fact, of course, he was born and brought up in Ballston Spa and had been taught English at the local school by the father of my ex-cohabitee. I was slightly annoyed, since my Antarctic dream had not included pointless coincidences that would make anyone feel we had something in common. It was already not solitary enough. Not lolloping, lonely Less Big Jim's fault though.

While all these Jims were going on, we were flying over or waiting in as godforsaken a landscape as God ever forsook. Looking down, across Big Jim's amazing belly, for hours as far as the eye could see there was nothing but grey-green scrubby flatness. I'd seen photos of the moon that had more personality. We flew for several hours over this entirely featureless landscape. This was nowhere to a degree I'd never experienced. Not white, perhaps, but borderless and blank. Not even the sea provides such uneventful stillness. Then suddenly we descended to Rio Gallegos airport in the middle of this nothingness, a few buildings surrounded by the absence of anything. Rio Gallegos is famous actually. Butch Cassidy and the Sundance Kid held up a bank there after they fled south from their dogged pursuers. Inconceivable that there could be a bank here, but now there is an airport and an espresso coffee machine and planes taking off to deliver people hundreds of miles this way and that to the nearest other towns in the middle of nothing.

Apart from some scrappy hills that seemed to have given up the effort – doubtless the ones that Butch and Sundance hid in with their loot (what did they spend the money on?) –

45

what there is in Rio Gallegos is wind. A special kind of Patagonian, end-of-the-world wind that introduced itself as we climbed out of the plane and walked across to the airport building. It whistled and flung itself at us like a slap on the back. The kind of wind you could dance with if only the music it made were more tuneful. This wind is not an inter-mittent thing. It is unceasing. It is the nature of Rio Gallegos. It blows and rushes, whistles and whines across the flat end-less plain of Patagonia, and if you get in its way you hold it up just enough to feel how far it's been and how far it's got to go, and how little difference the handful of buildings or you in its path is going to make. No fluttering butterfly wing would have a chance here to make its mark on the global weather system. The Patagonian wind has got turbulence wrapped up.

'Gee, that's a *hell* of a wind,' said Less Big Jim, hanging on to his baseball cap as we battled our way to the plane that would take us to Ushuaia. And he was right.

After an early dinner – almost a high tea – with Mona, I sat in my room at the Hotel Glacier, in the foothills above the town of Ushuaia, with my feet on the sill of the open window, staring at the eponymous glacier, half a mile away. I don't think I'd ever seen a glacier before, and I didn't see much of this one, just a slick of corrugated gleaming white in a dip in the mountain above us. Still, there it was, and I was looking at it, which was about as much excitement as I could manage just then. The hotel was familiar enough; a cross between a Swiss chalet and a Holiday Inn, wood-framed with those modular plastic bathrooms they probably drop in all in one piece: bath, plumbing, mock-marble sink surround, complimentary soap and all. It was fiendishly heated, which is why I had the window open. The air coming into the room was nothing more than refreshing despite being on latitude 56°S, which was as far south as I'd ever been, though not as far south as I was going.

I sat and stared, limp with travel fatigue and feeling slightly demented, deeply ashamed of my lack of inner resources, especially since Mona, who was ancient, was as frisky as a mayfly when I left her after our meal. Staring at the glacier was step two in my mental health recuperation programme. First, a long bath, two aspirins, a sleeping pill and the miniature Scotch Mona gave me because she prefers sherry but the stewardess didn't have any, so gave her a bottle of Bells instead; then sit with my feet on the windowsill in knickers and T-shirt, gazing at the undemanding glacier. Finally, step three, slip into bed and sleep away the unsettling sense of being still in transit in spite of having left home what felt like aeons ago. I wanted to get to where I was going, which to my mind at this point was the ship, specifically my cabin on the ship. I wanted to be there like a mole wants to be in its dark hole underground. It was all I wanted. My cabin was my only goal: Antarctica, whatever I was going to see of it, wasn't currently in the frame, but there was still most of tomorrow in Ushuaia to get through, since we weren't boarding until five in the afternoon. The ship was the *Akademik Vavilov*. As one might articulate the name of a beloved, I murmured its name to the glacier which absorbed it without hurry or surprise. Glaciers are useful like that, I discovered.

Next morning I was mended enough to go for an early walk towards the glacier before boarding the coach for the sightseeing tour of Ushuaia and its National Park. I didn't actually get to the glacier because I was waylaid by a wood, a dark green place, not dank and rotting underfoot like an English wood, but crisp and crackling because of the dry, near-freezing air. I hadn't gone very far before I found a dead furry thing lying in my path, eaten I suppose by some other larger furry thing. Since rabbits, guanaco and foxes are the only mammals in Patagonia, it should have been easy to figure out what the dead furry thing was, but it didn't look like anything that had once been a rabbit, and if it was a fox then it must have been cannibalized by one of its own; surely guanaco are vegetarian? Parts of it had been stripped to the bone; one leg, bent up, was just dry white tibia and fibula, but whatever had had its way with it must have had a small appetite because much of the rest was intact and quite cuddly-looking. It seemed that this far southern land was not just monumental snow-covered mountains, peaking at 5,000 feet and then dropping down towards the elegant sweep of the Beagle Channel, but that it harboured life that lived and died just like anywhere else. It surprised me, and then it surprised me that I should have imagined otherwise. I had only wanted landscape and here I was with companions, about to start a coach trip around Ushuaia, the town at the end of the world, and now even confronted by the evidence of mortality. I wasn't in search of the drama of life and death, but of what there is or isn't before and after. Changeless stuff. Empty stuff. Oblivion. It was, I remembered, as I stood looking at the dead furry thing in the woods below the glacier, immortal stuff that I was after.

There was nothing immortal about Ushuaia at first glance. It's a frontier city, a gold rush town where the gold is not in them there hills, but in the recent tax-free status conferred on it by the Argentinian government. What makes it remarkable is that it is the capital city of Tierra del Fuego, a land for most of us lodged in the imagination, just by the sound of the words, let alone the sense of its utter inaccessibility. It is the place where Robert FitzRoy, captain of the *Beagle*, and his dining companion, Charles Darwin, came to before journeying on to the Galapagos, and the place where the inhabitants convinced Darwin that they were earlier, primitive forms of the perfect men he and his countrymen had become. 'I would not have believed how entire the difference between savage and civilized man is. It is greater than between a wild and domesticated animal, in as much as in man, there is a great power of improvement.' FitzRoy put God to the test and brought three young Fuegians home with him, sent them to Sunday school, put them in gentlemen's and ladies' clothes and taught them table manners. These days some of the souvenir shops in the high street memorialize the most famous of these students of civilization, and call themselves Jemmy Button's. Even as Victorian experiments went, it wasn't a happy venture either for FitzRoy or the Fuegians.

49

The Fuegians who remained at home fared as poorly under the Argentinian government, as Tierra del Fuego became a territorial battleground between Argentina and Chile. In Darwin's day there were 10,000 Indians; by 1960 just 360; now, as you walk around, you see the merest hint in just a few of the faces. Chile and Argentina each claimed the land as theirs and went to war to prove it until a pope pontificated and created the present border line, or something quite like it. All this has something essential to do with oil and the fact that in the next twenty years or so the Antarctic Treaty will allow those with a handhold in the area to exploit the mineral resources. The finger of Tierra del Fuego and its nail of Ushuaia pointed firmly in the direction of Antarctica and its untouched hoard of mineral wealth. Not long ago the Chileans built Porto Williams just further enough south of Ushuaia, across the Beagle Channel, to cause the Argentinians to upgrade Ushuaia's already dubious status from a town to a full-blown city. Now they have the city at the end of the world, and just to make absolutely sure of the legitimacy of their claim, they have built a golf course. 'I've never seen anyone play golf there,' said our wry young tour guide, Stefan, who was born in Ushuaia. 'That's because no one in Ushuaia knows how to play golf, but now we have the golf course at the end of the world as well as the southernmost city.'

Tax-free status ensured Ushuaia's future as a boom town, with electronics manufacturers rushing to take advantage and mobile workers heading south for the soaring wages. 'People think you have to be rugged to live here,' said Stefan with an indolent shrug. 'But it's easy living here these days. We lose water and electricity sometimes, but that happens everywhere. Well, everywhere in Argentina. We get HBO, MTV and CNN. Just like anywhere else.' Stefan is a Fuegian with attitude, though I was sorry when he apologized to the British for the Falklands War, as we left the bus, and didn't wait for us to apologize in return.

As part of our tour, we visited the National Park which runs down to the Beagle Channel. 'We have something called Red Tide here,' Stefan warned. 'Don't even think of eating the mussels – fifteen minutes, and the game is over.' The National Park consists largely of vast old beaver dams, the constructors of which some merry missionary had brought in along with the rabbits and grey fox. Since none of them had any predators they thrived, and caused rabbit, beaver and grey fox havoc, the beaver dams being especially destructive of the landscape. Mostly, the beavers have been shot. There were no new beaver dams in sight, but the old, deserted ones were immense structures of etiolated logs criss-crossed over rivers and streams, beautiful and ghostly; adventure playgrounds that have lost their children. Stefan dutifully pointed out some of the bird species which form the real animal life of the archipelago. Great grebes, upland geese, kelp geese, sea snipe. Pretty names, but a load of ducks to me. Still, for all her bird weariness about the ubiquity of the species in the area, Mona bobbed up and down in the seat next to me pointing her binoculars this way and that as feathered flyers flashed past. Me, I was checking my watch to see how long it was until I got to my cabin, when some really interesting bird flapped by, so I missed it.

But I couldn't avoid the end of the road. It is specifically the end of Route 3, which begins in Alaska and wends its way down through North America and South America for 17,000 miles until it arrives at a wooden pontoon. Here I managed to spend a half hour or so dangling my legs over the Beagle Channel. Here I am, I thought, at the end of the world. In the Beagle Channel. Really, the *Beagle Channel*. I didn't know what to make of it, except that I shouldn't eat the mussels, but it was half an hour of peace and quiet, and for that I was grateful. The mouth of the Beagle Channel was a great glassy lake of gently rippling, steely blue-grey water. Only the occasional bird interfered with its stillness. Bright white clouds back-lit by the sun were surrounded by weighty rain clouds that gloomed the light but held on to their load of precipitation. In the distance, as I sat on the pontoon, a narrow passage of water between black rock, and further off, snow-covered peaks showed the direction we would be heading that night. The pontoon at the end of the world was not the end of the world. The world from here turned liquid and flowed, sometimes stormed, on south, and I was going in that direction. That was something.

The half-hour's privacy became addictive, and at lunch in the National Park's canteen at the end of the world I found a table to myself and buried my head in Bruce Chatwin's *In Patagonia*, to signal to my newfound friends that I didn't need company. That was when I met the cat at the end of the world, a long-haired, self-possessed fiery red Fuegian, fat on freely available duck and rabbit. It tapped me on the knee, pushed the book on my lap aside and, taking a minute or two to find the best angle, elongated itself comfortably along my thighs, purring like a coffee grinder. It didn't seem to mind being used as a book rest, so the Fuegian cat and I spent a contented hour, my second of the day, doubtless its umpteenth, appreciating each other's capacity for stillness. I would have settled for this. A couple of weeks sitting with the Fuegian cat, reading, drinking coffee, smoking and glancing out at the Beagle Channel, would have suited me fine. Like the best times of being at home, only with an upgraded view.

But lunch was over and we were invited to step back on the bus and experience Ushuaia town itself. I excused myself to the cat, which stretched and shrugged, then wandered off to find something else unexciting to do, while I reminded myself that I was supposed to be having an adventure and returned to the bus.

The town of Ushuaia is a collective act of imagination unhampered by planning constraints. Once, between 1902 and 1947, Ushuaia was a penal colony, just a place where Argentina sent its prisoners. The strangely high tree-line testifies to the hard labour they put in cutting down the trees to make their living accommodation, and when that was completed, just to be kept busy. Once Ushuaia became politically useful, the prison was closed, and people began to colonize the land for sheep farming and the greater glory of Argentina. Now, there is a main street and it's even got a name, San

Martin, but that's only because all Argentinian main streets are called San Martin. Duty-free electronic outlets and tourist shops filled with City at the End of the World knick-knacks line the street, along with a few restaurants and the occasional bakery. To some extent there is a pavement on the main street, though it is intermittent, and becomes rubble without warning or reason. The shop windows are dark and dismal, the goods crammed in, showing what's available, not inviting the pleasure of browsing and discovery. The shopping street is just an elongated warehouse, a practical sales outlet, devoted to shifting boxes of this and that. At the last count, in 1991, there were 29,464 inhabitants. Stefan, our guide, thinks this number may well have doubled.

The joy of Ushuaia is off the main street, up the steep hills behind the town, where crowding every inch beside the unmade roads are dwellings that would make the designers of Oz hearts sing. It seems if you do not tell people what kind of houses to build, or where to build them, they will put up remarkable and ridiculous structures: wood-framed triangles, rectangles with toytown roofs and soaring, unnecessary towers, and paint them higgledy-piggledy in the primary reds, blues and yellows of a child's paintbox. There are hovels and strange agglomerations of architecture. Houses like wedges of multilayered cake. Wood houses, concrete houses, even plastic houses and tents, all side by side. You see Ushuaia in all its congested, brilliant, absurd and taste-free glory, and laugh. Perhaps because it reminds you of the houses you built as a child with those brightly painted building blocks, triangular roofs, columns, elementary windows and spires, that came neatly packaged in a box, though not for long. Houses are squashed within inches of each other, some have just been thrown up, wooden frames criss-crossed with two-by-fours and covered with newspaper and polythene. Some are so small, they look like oversized dog kennels. Many of these houses are built on skids: as yet there are no planning regulations, but if city ordinances should come, these pioneers are ready for them, and will simply tow their houses somewhere else out of the planners' way. In the meantime, everywhere you look, houses are being constructed, and the sound of hammering, sawing and concreting fills the air along with dust and fumes from rusty cars that clatter around the stony roads.

On one edge of the town, the port is vivid and busy with boats coming and going to the South Atlantic, on the way to or from Antarctica with base camp personnel, or tourists, or fishing boats out for bottom-fish, a thriving new industry. There are science ships also trawling the cold sea for ice fish and measuring krill. There are supply ships. The rust-bucket fishing boats lie alongside the white cruising ships and the harbour is as lively as the streets with buying and selling and coming and going. On the other edge of the squash of human habitation are green swathed hills and behind them the white-topped La Martial mountains whose sharp peaks finish in the clouds. In between is the chaos at the end of the world. Just a bit of chaos between the sea and the mountains, but enough to give notice to the elements that civilization has arrived.

Everywhere, on the streets, in the harbour, around the houses, in and out of the shops, people in parkas are going somewhere in a hurry. They've all got business to conduct, things to sell, tourists to turn around, deals to close. This is Ushuaia, the southernmost city in the world. Ushuaia, from the German, thanks to the missionaries, meaning 'port facing the sunset'. This is hustlers' city, and it feels as vivid and vibrant as New York City or Las Vegas. It may be the most exciting place in the world. And now, please, *now*, is it time to get to the ship?

The distance between Ushuaia and Cabin 532 was one of those infinite distances proposed by science fiction writers who have their heroes cross galaxies by space-time warp; or that other, Victorian, distance depicted by Lewis Carroll when Alice climbs back through the Looking Glass into her drawing-room. Perhaps, for the rest of my fellow travellers, entering their cabins signified departure, but for me it was the moment of arrival, the very definition of the distinction between being not in the right place and arriving.

I had never been on a proper cruise ship, so there had been anxieties. Would I be troubled by someone's attempt to decorate the cabin into a similitude of a floating hotel? I feared a patterned carpet, curtains and bedding; those amorphous floral indications in vapid colours which are supposed to have the merit of not disturbing anyone while producing faint echoes of country-house comfort: the neither strident nor too plain effect produced by modern, modular hotels. I braced myself for disappointment as I opened the door, but found instead nine foot by seven and a half foot of wish-fulfilment.

The *Akademik Vavilov* was not, after all, originally intended as a cruise ship, and in its new role had not been made over to pretend to be one. Though the tour company was Canadian, its fleet of six ships were Russian-owned. *Vavilov* and her sister ships had been oceanographic research vessels, ice-hardened, for cruising the northern seas of the Arctic to make soundings, analyse weather patterns and examine the content of the seas. But science can no longer be paid for since the break-up of the USSR and in order to keep the ships and their crews afloat, they have leased them to the Canadian company as tourist vessels, equipped to carry up to seventy paying passengers. As a result, the cabins are designed for the basic comfort and efficiency of people with work to do, not for the hypothesized tastes of holiday-makers.

I don't think I have ever been in a room that contained nothing I did not want and everything I did. Even my own rooms lack that kind of purity. All sorts of objects find their way into the flat, things I once wanted and want no longer but haven't got round to throwing out; souvenirs that aren't looked at gather dust; Chloe's things (generally boots) and my things left where they were dropped and become part of the scenery of a room. Even my hallowed bedroom has mystifying corners of shoe aggregations, most of which will never be worn again but which somehow defeat my will to emptiness. And my small, white-tiled bathroom, intended as a shrine to minimalism, now sports a gilded cherub, a Christmas present from my daughter, casting a watchful, or possibly ironic eye at me from one corner of the mirror, to say nothing of half-unfinished bottles and tubes of cosmetics, shampoos and miracle-working unguents which, though disruptive of bathroom tranquillity, I keep on no firmer grounds than that I might, though I know I won't, use them up one of these days. I wouldn't call it chaos, indeed my more haphazard friends despair of my environmental control, but it isn't quite right.

Cabin 532 was quite as right as could be, and in recognition of this I let out a gasp and then laughed at the improbability of my being here, far from anywhere and entirely, at that moment, satisfied with my environment. Plain white walls, a desk, a book shelf above it, cupboards ranged along one wall with a small built-in fridge, a narrow wardrobe occupying the space between the end of the bed and the bathroom, deep shelves above the bed, and a tiny bathroom in which no kitten could swing, with a drain hole in the floor that turned it into a shower room with a flick of the plain plastic curtain. The bed was a wooden-sided bunk built along the wall opposite the desk, with a pair of beige curtains running across it to close it off from the rest of the cabin. The bedding, to my delight, was all white. Sheet, pillow cases and thin padded duvet, neatly folded and ship-shape. White, all white. Opposite the door was a large rectangular window – porthole, if you must – which opened wide. Nothing else. It was a monk's cell. Not the medieval version which I knew would be too physically rigorous for my gratification-seeking soma, but a modern version, for a latter-day monk spoiled by central heating and the pleasures of square feather pillows, with an effete belief that the workings of the mind are enhanced by the comfort of the body.

I opened the window and settled in. Plugged in my computer, put papers in the desk drawer, books on the shelf, and unpacked my clothes, which stowed away in the narrow wardrobe and plentiful cupboards, leaving the room almost as empty as I had found it, except for the encouragingly purposeful laptop and books which proclaimed the cabin my workspace and helped to justify the howling sense of well-being I experienced as I stood in the middle of the room I would be living in for the next fortnight.

Immediately, with that thought, there was a pang. Why only a fortnight? I snuffed out the flashing image of two weeks hence and me disembarking, already an ex-passenger. That time-murdering technique which I find most useful when waiting in anxiety for the daughter's key in the lock late at night, or fast-forwarding to the completion of a manuscript that seems to be frozen in its progress, turns and bites me – it is always and indiscriminately at the ready – with the gobbling up of the best of times, so that even in anticipation it seems that good things might as well not happen at all, since already, in my mind's eye, they have passed and gone. The sense of peace at my perfect surroundings was replaced by a kind of panic, a sense of time running out, so I tried the other, less certain, technique of living in seconds, holding them, being aware of each, making time sticky with self-consciousness. It works quite well when you are alone and uninterrupted, but is hard to keep a grasp on once any kind of busyness occurs. We were to set sail, if that's what an engine-driven ship does, within the hour, then there would be a meeting, or, as we had been told over the loudspeaker, a briefing – in keeping with the expeditious tone of the advertising – shortly afterwards. I could have explored the ship, but decided to hang on to time for a while and lay myself down on the bunk. I considered drawing the bed curtains, but this seemed premature, and anyway I still had a sense that Sister Winniki was hovering about and would laugh me to scorn.

The Spanish sounds of Ushuaia docks wafted in through the open window and bursts of Russian came through the loudspeaker in my room as the captain told the crew to man the mainbraces or whatever captains tell their crew to do when preparing to get going. The noise of the world getting on with it at a distance enhanced my inactivity; my watching of empty space bounded by four walls and practical, fitted necessities. I looked with great care at nothing in particular and noted deliberately the nothing I was looking at. At this rate I would possess my cabin for an eternity.

Indolence has always been my most essential quality. Essential in the sense that it is the single quality I am convinced I possess and by which I can be recognized and remembered, and also in the sense that I feel most essentially like myself when I am exercising it. I cannot recollect a time when the idea of going for a walk was not a torment to me; a proposition that endangers my constant wish to stay where I am. I imagine myself, child and adult, curled up in an armchair, reading and being told (as a child) or invited (as an adult) to go out and do something. I cannot think why a person sitting with evident contentment in an armchair causes the desire in others for their immediate activity. As a child I would leave the flat when the cries became insistent and find a safe haven on the back stairs, or the furthest end of the corridor next to the bronze, latticed radiator, and resume my non-activity. As an adult, especially when visiting people, I used to make an effort, with considerable distress, put down my book, pull on jumpers, jacket and boots (it is always cold when visiting friends) and go for the proposed walk, every step of which seemed a terrible waste of good sitting time. These days, maturity has enabled me to say a firm *no, thank you* to the proposition. The aim on these walks is to get cold and damp and head for the pleasure of some cosy pub or café before setting off again into the cold and damp to return to the warm, satisfactory haven we had abandoned in the first place. I understand that people like to make distinctions, that to enjoy this they have to interrupt it with that, but I've never found it necessary. I cannot see the point of interrupting something which is going very nicely.

There is also the matter of landscape, the beauty of it, the freshness of the air, the sense of being part of the natural world – even the sense of being part of the urban world. I do like landscape, but I am quite content to watch it through a window while curled up in my armchair. I wholly approve of rooms with good views. As to the freshness of the air, I'm not so eager for it. Though it is invigorating I admit, I very rarely have the desire to be invigorated. With respect to being part of the natural or urban world, much of the time I know I am part of it, except when I am not sure, but I have not found that walking through a landscape or along a crowded street has ever firmed up my conviction in this area. I've lived long enough to know it is a fact that most people find activity useful and confirming, but I am not one of those people; on the contrary, I find it alarming and alienating. It's one reason why I am inclined to holiday alone, and why sharing a cabin, which would have been considerably cheaper, was out of the question. There were going to be enough activity demands on this trip without any cabin mate's chirpy invitation to rise from my bunk to get some fresh air and take a stroll around the deck. Just because I was making a voyage to the most inaccessible place on earth, I saw no call for chirpiness beyond the absolutely necessary.

Once the *Vavilov*'s engines began to hum underneath me and the ship slowly to move away from the dock, I had no choice but to recognize the inauguration of time. The commencement of the sea journey began a schedule which would tick away the trip, but more immediately it set a limit to my idling on the bunk. I soothed my anxiety at the inevitable interruption of my time-free moments with the promise of a return to the bunk at regular intervals. Holidays from the timetable. Though, of course, a timetabled holiday, fitting in with some larger schedule, is not the freedom from agenda I would like to enjoy. It's often been suggested to me that could I have such an existence, I would hate it, find myself bored, restless and aching to participate in the time-and-necessity

62

bound world. It's untestable to any real degree, since even I know that an agenda-free life is unachievable, that my desire to finish whatever tasks I have to do and then, finally, be free to do nothing ever again, is a fantasy, or at any rate a description of the state of being dead – always supposing that the rotting of my corpse won't feel like an interruption. But what I also know is that during such periods when I have experienced free-running, obligationless time, the boredom and restlessness that occasionally comes over me is curiously part of the pleasure, and not detrimental to my feeling of well-being at all. If it's not true that I am never bored, it seems to be the case that I don't mind being bored. And if some socialized fraction of my mind tells me that there is something amiss about finding boredom a more satisfying condition than the threat of activity, then I acknowledge it with no anxiety at all. Very probably, but still. Come a lonely, decrepit and isolated old age, I may discover I am wrong about this, that it is no more than a conceit supported by the impossibility of its achievement. Very possibly, but still. As things stand at present a phone call initiating activity is never so welcome as the one cancelling it. It's not routine as such that I cannot abide. There is a kind of intrinsic routine that is the very essence of satisfactory times. When I am alone, at home, I get up, work, eat, sleep, work, sleep, eat in a pleasurable round dictated by my physical needs. I'm hungry, I eat. I'm sleepy, I sleep. And work, especially the long haul of a full-length manuscript, is not an intrusion, but lives well enough with the physical requirements. Given a sunny holiday and no one suggesting walks, the day falls into gratifying folds of sun-worship, work, eating and sleeping, according to the dictates of the sun. I don't resent the needs of my body, nor the movement of the planet, and am quite prepared to live by their rhythms. It is external appointments, those made by people on other schedules that I find trying. I have lived by them and still do, but freedom from them is something I most viscerally desire. The moving of the *Vavilov* was the first phone call. *Soon* was set in motion. Soon we would be called to the briefing. Soon I would meet my fellow travellers and the regularity of our days would begin. There would be meals and lectures and landings. I lay on my bunk trying fiercely to hang on to the few moments left before it all began, but the fierceness itself ended the peace and I found I was already waiting for the next thing to happen.

The briefing was very like a first school assembly. The seventy passengers and seven expedition staff filled the meeting room entirely. We all meant to make a positive start, smiling and exchanging names until we were called to order by Butch, our leader (no, he wasn't really called that, but he'll always be Butch to me), standing at the front with the other expedition staff.

The Rules. *One hand for the ship* applied at all times: always keep a hand free to hang on to safety rails, inside and on deck. Get to meals on time. All wet gear was to be left in the Mud Room on Deck One: no muddy boots in corridors or cabins. During landings keep within sight of an expedition leader and return to the meeting place immediately if called. Never take anything, not a stone, not a discarded feather, from any of the landing places. Do not leave anything behind on land. Comply exactly with the crew's instructions and use the sailor's hand-shake – hands to wrists – when getting on or off the Zodiacs (the black rubber motorized dinghies on which we would go ashore). We were welcome to go at any time to the bridge, but we must keep our voices down and not interfere with the work of the Russian crew on watch.

Butch was a tall, thick-necked American with a walrus moustache and a deep, sonorous voice, whose brow knitted when he spoke, as if he were configuring his sentences before allowing them out into the air. Language did not come easily to Butch. His leadership qualities did not include concision. 'The Zodiacs were somewhat developed, designed, invented by a fellow you may have heard of – Jacques Cousteau. They are entered into by way of the gangway.' 'The lifejacket is a flotation device.' 'Your interests vary considerably with why you are going ashore.' We got all the information we needed but wrapped in a caul of language that made it hard to con-centrate on what rather than how it was said. There was something touching about the ponderous Butch, the man of action tangled up in words. The eyes of the rest of the expe-dition crew were veiled, but one or two failed to conceal their impatience completely.

As Butch talked, the ship beneath us began to feel quite lively, rocking up and down as it met the open waters of the Drake Passage. It wasn't anything dramatic, nothing a regular sailor would notice, but for me it was a moment of realization:

we were really at sea, really travelling over the capricious surface of fathoms of water. Butch informed us, as a murmuring
went up at the stronger movement, that we were on the most
unpredictable seas on the planet, and in the next couple of
days we might find ourselves being 'somewhat bounced
around'. We should be prepared and stow everything movable
away in cupboards and drawers that night, as things were
expected to get quite sparky by one o'clock the next morning.
The briefing, belying its name, finished just before 7 p.m.
when a lifeboat drill was scheduled. We returned to our cabins
to retrieve our lifejackets from the drawers under our bunks
and wait for the alarm, before congregating at our designated
lifeboat stations.

The two orange lifeboats were like miniature submarines,
not the open rowing boats of the movies and more temperate
seas. In the event of an unscheduled meeting with an iceberg,
we would put on all our warmest clothes and calmly assemble
to bundle into their empty dark interiors and close the hatch.
In these seas, a human body in the water would last about ten
minutes before hypothermia set in.

'They've got a back-up system,' I heard a voice behind me
say as we trooped back inside. 'Go and check it out on the deck
below.' I turned to see a spare, rather tall, grey-haired woman
with sparkling blue eyes. Beside her, a smaller, slighter,
bearded man with remarkably similar lively eyes was chuckling. They were both in their mid-sixties, he was perhaps a
little older than her. They had been making jokey asides
during the lifeboat drill about the likelihood of surviving in

those roofed buckets. I took a liking to the pair, especially the woman, to their accents and loud, raucous voices, to the dryness of their humour, and to, for all their spry outdoor fitness, their urbanity. I felt comfortable, as I hadn't done since the trip began, with their style, which was recognizable as New York Jewish. When I made for the lower deck I saw a white, rusting, decrepit Volkswagen Golf roped incongruously to the railings.

After depositing my lifejacket back in its drawer, a cheery voice over the loudspeaker announced that the bar was open for drinks before dinner. I headed down two flights to the dining room and found the bar already crowded with people making each other's acquaintance. Daniel the barman mixed me a Manhattan, cooled with chips from a hunk of glacier ice taken on board at Ushuaia. He was already in full flow, explaining to Big Jim that he was an actor from Toronto. He signed on for the trip, he said, because he was in love. 'Like joining the Foreign Legion?' I wondered. 'Oh no, she loves me, too. We are in love.' The open-faced romance of young Daniel was a sight to be seen. Dreamy-eyed, he told us of the beauty and grace of his beloved, who was an Argentinian from Buenos Aires. Somehow, bartending in the Antarctic Ocean was the way he found to be near her – though the distance from Buenos Aires to the Antarctic Peninsula might be almost as far as the distance from Canada. 'I write to her every day, sometimes twice a day,' Daniel glowed, shaking and mixing drinks for the next customer. 'Of course, I can't post them until we get to South Georgia and then again when I'm back in

Ushuaia, but I wouldn't feel happy unless I wrote to her before I went to bed.' As I wandered off, sipping a good enough Manhattan, I hoped Daniel's beloved knew what a treasure she had. Then I wondered whether it wouldn't be better if she didn't realize. Sometimes, treasures can be a terrible burden. I decided to suppose that Daniel's beloved was not in any way like myself, and that it was all as delightful as it sounded, and they would live to a happy and contented old age. After which I confined my romantic notions to the idea and practice of drinking a Manhattan made with glacier ice.

I passed Less Big Jim and smiled hello, but was deflected by the sight of the Jewish couple from the lifeboat drill, sitting in a corner seat beside the bar, and I made my way towards them, receiving a warm welcome when I asked if the space beside them was free. 'Did you see the back-up life-saving system?' Emily asked me with a smile. 'As the ship starts sinking, we jump in and drive like hell,' said Manny, throwing his head back, roaring with laughter. I was pleased they were on the boat and that I had come across them on the first evening.

Emily and Manny had been disputatiously married for forty-five years. Argumentation was their mode; whatever one of them said, the other contradicted or provided a public commentary upon. They had been engaged in a lifelong battle with each other. For the duration of Happy Hour I enjoyed their bantering, zesty discord, their commitment to contention.

'Ach, he's such a sourpuss,' Emily told me as Manny disparaged the bourgeois appearance of our fellow passengers. 'He's a lot older than me.'

'She's no chicken. She's got to argue with me. She's got to feel she's right.'

'He's always got to have the last word.'

'Well, it's always a good word.'

'Mouth. Mouth. Mouth.'

All of this between chatter about where we were from, why we were here. It was a private duet between them which had spread across the boundaries of privacy. There was a bounciness to it that relieved my onlooker's embarrassment and let me enjoy the entertainment I was being offered. For the moment I chose not to think about the accumulation of forty-five years of mutual dissent, or to wonder what the private face of this comic war might be, and just enjoyed the performance. I was an outsider and not obliged to absorb whatever pain went along with all this. Though he tried too hard and began to make me a bit uneasy, I was attracted to the couple, not just for their entertainment value, but also for an unexamined notion I had of the possibility of their combativeness as a bond of affection between them. Somehow it seemed more possible, even more desirable, as a way of companionship than Daniel's sojourn in the world of marshmallow-hued romantic love.

I am not unaware of being drawn to unfamiliar couples a generation or so older than myself, people of a parental age, who to a stranger, seem to have negotiated years together and come to an accommodation with each other. I watched this tendency in myself when I spent a couple of weeks on a minuscule Caribbean island a few years back. They were in the cabin next door to mine, French and in their sixties too, quiet and contented-seeming. We never spoke, though we smiled good morning and shared silent astonishment and pleasure one afternoon at a huge iguana sun basking between our cabins. Once when a multisailed beauty of a yacht glided past, he passed me his binoculars as we stood and watched its silky progress. Every morning, after breakfast, I made my way across the island, equipped with book, suntan lotion and portable CD-player, to an out-of-the-way beach for solitary sun worship and sea staring. The French couple, arriving after me on the island, found this beach too, and shared it, spreading their towels a good non-disturbing distance from my pitch. We waved to each other on their or my arrival, and as we left the beach. No one else ever came, except to look and pass on. I enjoyed their distant company, as if they confirmed and endorsed my pleasure in idling the hours away. I liked what I imagined was their approval and the non-invasive mutual smiles and pointing gestures when a wonderful long-necked bird landed on the beach between us. Before they left they came to my cabin and said goodbye, and we congratulated each other on having been highly satisfactory neighbours. Their absence from the beach the following day disturbed me. Not that I minded being alone but it did become clear how much I had invested in them as distant, approving parental figures, liking me and letting me be. I missed them, and felt a little foolish for growing a pair of fantasy 'good' parents in the world beyond my psyche. Too needy, I thought, but then no harm had been done. Nothing wrong with missing people, even if they were the wrong people, since I hadn't tangled myself up in their lives.

Emily and Manny Roth were not just the connected older couple I liked to imagine, but lively and verbal, and Jewish too. Not surprising that I found them alluring. But over dinner my fantasies disintegrated. Although I had got no nearer to them than across the table, I had stepped closer than my fragile fantasy could stand. I learned the value of the silence and space I kept between myself and my Caribbean beach dream-parents.

The Roths had lived for years in Santa Fe.

'What do you do?' I asked.

'I'm a fighter,' Emily snapped back. 'I've brought up two kids, and I don't do anything except fight where the fighting needs fighters.'

'Boy, is she ever a fighter,' Manny groaned, though his voice was tinged with pride.

'What do you fight?'

'Everything. I just love fighting. I like the hand-to-hand battles. I'm a real street-fighter, and I haven't mellowed, but now I'm sixty-five, I find I worry about getting my teeth knocked out and my eyesight damaged. I'm more careful than I used to be. I'm getting tired. These days I focus my fighting around our community.'

Amused and intrigued by the fierce, over-dramatic description of herself, I supposed this was political commitment, and imagined street demonstrations during the civil rights battles, the Cold War, the Rosenberg executions; anti-McCarthy,

71

anti-Vietnam, the plight of Mexican immigrants. I was correct about the political commitment, but entirely deluded as to its nature.

'Yes,' Emily continued with a sigh. 'These days I just write letters and lobby the government about the welfare being poured into the Indians and all those endless children they breed. The big battle we've won already. The fight against the Communists, getting our people out of the Soviet Union.'

'Our people?'

'The Jews. Getting the Jews out of Russia, back home.'

'Home?'

'Israel. Where else is home?'

I could see how you might combine demanding the rights of Soviet Jews to emigrate with anti-Vietnam and civil rights demonstrations, but the reference to the Indians indicated another sort of agenda. My spirit sinking, I opted, initially, for clarification on the marginally less troubling option.

'You're Zionists, then?'

'Zionists, and well to the right of Attila the Hun on all things political,' Emily replied proudly, answering both my asked and unasked questions with the relish of a born-again street-fighter ready for an argument. 'We're followers of Kahane. Boy, did we celebrate when we heard that Rabin had been assassinated. He was asking for it. No one wanted him in power except the Arabs and a few Socialists.'

Rabbi Meir Kahane was a Brooklyn Jew who founded the Jewish Defence League, an ultra-orthodox, militant funda-mentalist group whose aim is to return all Jews to Israel. He was assassinated in 1990, after a lifetime of abusing Arabs, blacks and any Jews who had assimilated with other cultures. The latter most of all. At a memorial service for Kahane in Jerusalem, after Yitzhak Rabin's assassination, Kahane's followers calculated the numbers of the assassin's name according to the kabbala, believing they would add up to 'Messiah'.

'Israel is the Jewish homeland,' explained Manny, seeing dismay on my face.

'Not for me.'

'Then you're not a Jew,' Emily said, rather gently. 'You're in denial. You're a Jew who has lost her meaning.'

'You're not a Jew at all,' insisted Manny.

'You are lost,' Emily told me sadly.

'But why do you live in Santa Fe? Why not in Israel?'

They had. They had emigrated to Israel, but it didn't work out. They returned to the US after two years.

'Why?'

'We couldn't stand all the Jews there,' Manny grinned and then hooted with laughter.

'But we flew to Israel when the scuds were being dropped. To be with our people in their time of trouble.'

I was very disturbed by the Roths. But oddly, I still found Emily attractive, in spite of loathing her opinions. She was easier to be with, less messianic sounding, warmer, but I suspected she was actually the more fanatical of the two. Of course, Emily wasn't brought up a practising Jew. I longed for the meal to be over, because I had a feeling I only knew the

73

half of what they believed, and I didn't want them to tell me the rest. As far as they were concerned, I was a lost Jew, and that must have seemed as ugly to them as they appeared to me. I wondered if, despite my dismay at their views, I none the less wanted their approval. The parent thing again, and nothing to do with what they or I thought about anything. I felt discouraged, by them and by myself.

At last dinner was over, though I couldn't scurry back to my cabin until Butch had made yet another welcoming speech and introduced us to our captain who sat at the corner table with some of his officers. Captain Kalashnikov, very short, but every inch a captain in his nifty uniform, stood and bowed solemnly. That done, Butch handed out the next day's itinerary. The sheet was headed with a thought for the day. Masefield: *I must go down to the seas again, to the lonely sea and the sky* . . . Breakfast at eight. At ten, a lecture on Antarctica and the Subantarctic islands. Lunch at twelve. Another lecture at two, entitled, ominously 'Life at Sea. Is it for the Birds?'. At four, tea and snacks. Happy Hour began at six, dinner was at eight and to end the day a video of *The Fugitive* would be shown. Did I say I felt a timetable coming on? I panicked slightly, wondering how I would fit in lying in my bunk and staring out to sea. But at least I could now return to Cabin 532.

It was about 9.30 in the evening and still light. Investigating my corridor, I found a door at the far end and beyond it a small open deck with a couple of benches. A solitary spot in the open for sitting and staring. The wind was as strong as a fist, and the sea, under an eggshell grey sky, was an effulgent blue, like the contents of a bottle of royal blue ink, quinky blue, and choppy. Small waves curled on the surface topped with frothing whitecaps. But beneath the busy movement, the substance of the sea seemed profoundly deep and massively still, as though what went on at the surface was of no concern to it. Apart from the wind, it wasn't very cold. There was nothing out there, just an arc of horizon, as I leaned over the railing on one side, then the other and turned to look behind me. We really were in the middle of nowhere and there was nothing but sea and sky as far as the eye could reach. Not white, but real emptiness. I unshrivelled a little from my evening with the Roths, as I gazed at the expanse and recollected that we had three full days of this. Our first stop was to be at South Georgia, 800 miles to the south east of Ushuaia, and there was not a thing between, only sea, sky and space. At this point on the planet you could travel its span without bumping into a single piece of land before returning to where you started. It's the cause of the winds and storms that whip up tempests in these latitudes; there's nothing to stop them rolling around the world picking up velocity like an ice skater. I was in no hurry to see land. In fact, I rather dreaded the idea of the ship stopping, of having to get off it and explore. But three days of travelling on water seemed luxuriously long enough to put thoughts of land out of my mind. I was beguiled by the sea and so much of it; snow and ice and white places were in abeyance for the time being.

An hour or so later, I returned to my bunk, got under the thin duvet and watched the sky outside my porthole for a bit, before opening the copy of *Moby Dick* I had brought with me on the grounds that now, if ever, was the time to overcome my aversion to nautical literature. By the third page I was thrumming with pleasure at the energy and freedom of Melville's writing, but by midnight, though it was still silvery light outside, I was bleary from the unfamiliar sea air and probably from my alarming encounter with the Roths, and I slept.

Suddenly, I was instantly wide-eyed awake. It had to be morning, because the cabin was light. But the clock read 1.30 and though, if I had been in London it could have been an average overcast lunchtime and I'd outrageously overslept, it was actually the middle of a southern summer night. I hadn't closed the curtains by the bed so the lack of darkness must have filtered into my brain and confused it into preparing for a new day. I got up and looked out to see still nothing but endless sea, to my relief. I liked the strangeness of this unending daylight and my disoriented physiology. I read for a while and then slept again, but not for long. I was fully awake again at 3.30 and ready for the day to start, but now I just lay in my bunk and became aware of the change that had come over the movement of the ship, and the movement of myself with it.

The rolling had begun in earnest and the ship was pitching up and down, not roughly, but in a prolonged surging rhythm. My bunk was at right angles to the length of the ship, so that I felt the stern to bow rocking laterally, across my body, like being swayed from side to side in a hammock. It was a kind of dance my body was doing to the music of the ship, which itself was dancing to the rhythm of the sea. A three-part syncopation: the sea, the ship and me, moving separately but in tune. With concentration, I could isolate the movement of each of those elements, feeling one of them as central, then another. When I focused particularly on the movement of my body and let sea and ship fade into the background, it felt like I was drifting gently, unaided, through the air, the way the sea birds do, catching billows of wind, rising on one and then falling on to the next, which lifts them up again.

Then I let myself become aware of the various levels that were causing my movement – my bunk, the ship, the depths of the sea – until I was being rocked by the planet itself, by the moon too, I suppose, just visible in the daylit sky, since its pull also excites the tidal movements I was experiencing. This was not a stormy sea, I knew, nothing like the most violent moments the Drake Passage can provide. There was a mellowness to the up and down movement of the ship, which translated into the side to side rolling in my bunk. Every now and then the ship was caught by a swell against its bows and it rolled and dipped from side to side, making my movement change so that I was rocked head to foot rather than side to side. And sometimes the ship ducked steeply as some larger wave hit, and there was a sharp bucking motion, that caused my viscera to take on a movement of their own, adding another level to those to which I was already paying attention. For a while I lay still and tried to make some pattern out of the various rockings: the internal rhythm that accorded with the rhythm of the ship that accorded with the rhythm of the sea. Perhaps it was like riding a horse. It was the most pleasing, utter contentment doing this, or not doing this, just lying there with a smile on my face and taking pleasure in the daylight in the middle of the night on the ocean.

My time in the Hove hospital was during the winter and I spent hours sitting on the empty pebbled beach watching the sea, gulls swooping, snow falling, wind whipping up the waves. Bodies of water hypnotize me. Bodies in water please me, too. Baths are only peripherally about getting clean; I bathe to restore mental and physical comfort to myself. Sitting in warm water improves my life like little else. And bodies on water. In sunny places, I can spend the best part of a day floating on an airbed right at the surface of the sea, letting the waves carry me in to shore, paddling myself out again with my arms and bobbing on the swell. That's as close as I've ever come to the pleasure I felt lying in my bunk cruising through the Drake Passage. Of course, there was that other kind of watery floating – suspended in amniotic fluid in the womb, where maternal movement must cause small surges to rock and sway you. I wondered that I had never thought about the fact of my mother – *my* mother – as my gestation site. I must have, of course, but would have slid away from the idea as being so unlikely, so improbable. However, the nature of the origins of my current shipboard pleasure, my amniotic fancies, was inescapable. I've tried to avoid the unavoidable conclusion all my life: always happier to imagine I was a foundling, an alien even, than to suppose that I spent nine warm contented months in my mother's uterus. That my first comfort was from within her body. Her body nurturing me. It came to me as an incredible thought, but the strength and sensuality of my delight at being on the ocean made it certain. It must have been nice in there. I didn't know my mother then. My mother didn't know how badly things were going to work out for her. Both of us innocent and ignorant. A good time, probably. But the idea of my mother, the mother I knew, nurturing me inside her body, as a reality made me dizzy.

As did, my mother coming to mind, the possibility – in fact, the probability if I were to be honest – that I would shortly find out after thirty years whether my mother was alive or dead. Since Chloe mentioned the death certificate she found, I'd brought both superpositional possibilities of my mother to the front of my mind once or twice and tried to make each of them real, but all that happened during my concentration on the notion of her being alive, was the sort of vertigo I was currently feeling at the idea of being my mother's foetus: a dizziness in my head and in my solar plexus as if I was standing on a high place looking down. At the idea of her being dead, I could not summon a single thought, not the hint of a feeling. I suppose when someone hasn't been around for a very long time, it's hard to feel anything about the continuation of their absence, even if their condition is altered by non-existence. Just more of the same. Only more certain. But common popular psychology told me there must be some feeling attached to the positive news of the death of my mother. Not a thing. Then again, there wasn't, so far, *positive* news of

79

her death. I told myself that I really ought to try harder, and have some thoughts, even a feeling or two about my mother and her possible non-existence or otherwise, but since I didn't seem to know how to know what I thought, let alone know how to feel what I felt, I decided, like Scarlett O'Hara, to leave it till another day.

Immediately, the dizziness disappeared and I was once again deliciously on my floating bed, absolutely where I wanted to be. And for three days I could be. I would read, I would lie in bed and from time to time go out on deck and up to the bridge, to take a look at how things are out there beyond my window; to see where we were, not that it mattered, but I wanted to pinpoint myself on the map. The sky beyond my window was occluded with dove-grey cloud and all I could see was a shadowed white out there, unless I raised myself up, and then I would see the inky sea and shadowed white. The horizon was a very long way away.

MRS ROSEN:	Often over the years we used to say . . .
MR ROSEN:	. . . Oh that poor girl.
MRS ROSEN:	. . . No, we used to say, what happened to Jennifer?
MR ROSEN:	Yes, many times, what happened to Jennifer? There's a nice title for you.

I remember Jennifer with about the same clarity that I remember the young Jane Eyre, Mary from *The Secret Garden*, Peter Pan and Alice. Rather less clarity, in fact, since the last four are readily available on my bookshelves and I have reacquainted myself with them quite regularly. Jennifer, I've merely remembered from time to time over an increasing distance of years, and with each remembering, each re-remembering, the living, flesh-and-blood fact of her slips incrementally from my grasp. As a person, she is far less substantial than Tinkerbell, who can be brought back into existence through the will of others. Jennifer does not light up when I clap my hands in recollection; she retains only a dim inner illumination. She did not even preserve her name until very recently.

The thing about Jennifer is that there has been no corroborating evidence for her existence these past thirty years, as there has been for the child characters in books I once read and can continue to read. There are no pictures, no written words, no other person who, remembering her, has spoken to me of her. She has existed exclusively inside my head, only exiting into the world like characters (of whom sometimes she is one) in the novels I write. She is no more certain than any other figment of my imagination. I might have made her up – I did make her up from time to time.

As a writer, there is considerable freedom in the vagueness of Jennifer. The child who often appears in my novels sometimes has experiences I remember, but frequently she doesn't. I am not fettered by history, by an absolute sense of telling-the-truth or making-things-up. I'm free to play around with who Jennifer was, might have been, never could have been. Sometimes it seems that I can get closer to her, or an essence of her precisely because of the distance between us. In any case, fiction is a funny business. When I have used actual events that occurred during my childhood – or my adulthood, come to that – the mere act of writing them and including them in a fiction, quite apart from altering them according to the needs of the book, separates them from the memorized event. Once it is written, I possess two distinct memories: the original event, intact, and, as I feel it, about me; and the written one, existing in parallel, vividly pictured but about the character I have created. So if the Jennifers I write into my fictions are me, they are proliferated mes; mes with their own autonomy – at least within the confines of their story. Jennifer, the faded child, remains as faded as ever. There is nothing new about the multiple versions of Jennifer. Much of my time as a child was spent in telling myself stories. The heroines and heroes I invented at the centre of these tales were me but not me. They had their own names, different ages, quite different circumstances. They lived out intricately detailed adventures and romances, as well as wishful thinkings. There were, I think, always fictional Jennifers.

Jennifer began to fade in 1966 when my father died and my mother disappeared. After that there was no one I knew who had known her, apart from myself. Perhaps the fading was not the first thing that happened. Jennifer became detached, became a separate character, someone with a story of her own. Although intellectually I knew that she and I were one and the same, emotionally she grew distant, acquiring a complete and finished life of her own, related structurally to me but existentially separate. I could recollect her environment with a greater clarity than I could her lived experience. I knew stories about her, incidents that had occurred in her life and I could review them as a series of tableaux, but she was a separate incarnation, not a present remembering self. They say the body undergoes a complete cell change every seven years, and this felt true to me. Jennifer inhabited her own existence, physically other, not me, not part of the continuum of me. I had to doubt the thoughts I thought I remembered her having, even the feelings; perhaps my remembering of Jennifer was like the animation of a puppet, my present retrospection pulling her strings and seeming to bring her to life. Who knows what Jennifer was like, with only memory as a guide?

My picture of any event occurring to Jennifer always includes Jennifer in the frame. The image is not from her eyes – which would be how a 'real' memory should be recalled, if such a thing as a 'real' memory could be said to exist – but seen from the outside, from some eyes beyond the frame and therefore – unless they are God's – not actually present at the time of the event. Treacherous, if there is no one to confirm or deny the facts of the event. 'I' seem to be remembering an occasion which I, as someone six times seven self-annihilating years removed from Jennifer, could not possibly have witnessed. Jennifer witnessed and participated in the event, but now she has become part of the image and not the seeing eye she must originally have been. Who is remembering what? When I think of Jennifer sitting on her father's lap, I see the back of Jennifer, her arms squeezing tight around a silver-haired, moustached, handsome man who is laughing and teasing her. What the hell I was doing there (if that actual moment ever existed and is not just a representation of a general memory), standing to one side, at a little distance from the armchair the two of them are sitting in, no more substantial than a pair of observing and possibly ironic eyes, I cannot say. Jennifer was frightened of ghosts. Perhaps she had every right to be.

Jennifer lived in mortal terror of ghosts. In the dark of night, they lived in closed cupboards, under beds, in dim corners and recesses, behind closed curtains. During the day, they were around the wrong corridor, behind unopened doors, came towards her in echoing footsteps on the granite stairs, were always standing behind her if her back wasn't to the wall. They were classical monsters, these ghosts, not fairy spirits, but ugly malicious beasts who bore ill will to small girls. They liked to pounce, screeching, with long stiletto nails to claw the flesh and sharpened teeth to rip it. They were the huge, misshapen mythic creatures that belong in all our psyches from god knows where or when. They hated Jennifer, though impersonally; they hated all small children and lay in wait for them. Jennifer maintained a vigil at nights watching the dark line between the cupboard door and the jamb, waiting for it to creak open and reveal the murderous contents. She would lie in bed and feel through her spine the presence of the horror which lived under her in the space between the bottom of the divan and the carpet, knowing it would slither out when all was quiet and terrorize her to death. Sometimes she lay for an hour or two, rigid with fear, but eventually she did what she knew she had to do. She got out of bed, slowly, very quietly, and got down on her hands and knees to examine the space under the bed. Then she went to the cupboard and, heart pounding, yanked the door fully open. This was the only power she had over the ghosts. Confronting them always made them disappear. But she knew they would be back. On a bad night she would have to get up four, five or six times before she finally allowed herself to fall asleep. You made the ghosts go away by looking at them, but it was an ongoing battle and, for Jennifer, the nightime rituals were lonely and shameful. She was ashamed because although she knew in her very marrow that the monsters were there, as well as she

85

knew that her parents were in the other room because they were shouting at each other, she also didn't believe in them. She lived with them, in mortal fear of them, but she knew, too, that they didn't really exist. It made them, of course, all the more fearful and all the more alarming. It made her all the more singular in her own existence, battling bravely with what was never there, fighting shadows that mocked her with their insubstantiality.

Strange times, night times. Apart from the ghosts, there were the shouting parents. Not every night – surely not. But memory does not stretch to nights without them shouting in the other room. Sometimes they actually fought and the sound of scuffling would echo through the flat. She would threaten to take an overdose. 'Take some for me,' he would say. Accusations, hatred, despair came through loud and clear – I always had the door open a crack. I needed the chink of light to check on the ghosts; I also needed to know how my parents' evening was going. Apart from ghost hunting, I did ritual magic at night. With the sound of their arguments in the background, I would draw a Star of David on my chest (Christians could cross themselves, I couldn't see why I shouldn't Star of David myself) and say 'Please' to God, asking him to stop the fights. I had to say please a hundred times, and if I lost count I'd have to start again. I never got to sleep early, it took a long time to complete the ritual. Sometimes I would find myself wishing differently – wishing, or praying to the same God that my parents would die, or that my real parents would come and collect me. Then I'd be obliged to say 'sorry' a hundred times, even though I wasn't sorry, just guilty. Occasionally, in an attempt to speed things up, I would cross myself instead of drawing the Star of David. I had a feeling that the cross was more kosher, might be more effective. But guilt again would demand that I then draw the Star of David one hundred times as penance for my heresy. Night times were busy. I failed to acquire the habit of easy sleep. That my parents never stopped arguing, never actually died, and no one ever came to claim me, didn't deter me from my rituals, good and bad. It was, I thought, only a matter of accumulating enough 'Pleases' or 'Sorries'. As a small child, I was dogged in my faith.

Once I gave it five minutes' practical thought, it was as easy to get access to the corridors of Paramount Court, about which I had been dreaming for so long, as it was to find the birth and marriage certificates of my mother. I phoned the head porter and explained that I had once lived there and was now want- ing to write about the place. A 'to whom it may concern' letter of my bona fides from my publisher clinched it.

'You won't be knocking on any doors, will you?' he asked when I arrived. 'We've got a lot of old people here.'

I explained it was just the corridors I was after, but while I was standing in his office, I noticed a board on the wall with the names of the occupiers of each flat. The names Rosen and Levine jumped out at me. They were the surnames of two of the children I played with in the flats, Jonathan and

Helen. As I waited for the lift to take me to the third floor, I noted down the names, a little surprised at remembering them and the faces of Jonathan and Helen so clearly after more than thirty years. It seemed to me incredible that their parents could really be living in the same place. Who stayed in one spot all that time? No one I ever knew. But I jotted the names down anyway.

I stepped out of the lift at the third floor, where we had first lived in the block, and walked directly into my memory. My recollection of the corridor had been exact, pale walls, pale patterned carpet, the large window beside the lift with horizontal bars from which I used to hang and swing, and from which I could look out to the fire escape and alleyway, where Jonathan or Helen or Susan would stand and signal secret messages to me. I walked in the carpeted silence, small murmurings of television and radio from behind the closed doors on either side, to the end of what still seemed a very long corridor to number 38, our flat, just before the entrance to the back stairs. At the very end there was the bronze, latticed cover to the radiator under the far window that I sat against for hour on hour reading and inventing private games. I wandered back down and walked the corridor on the second side of the building, turning that dangerous corner I only turned as a child when I was feeling brave. It felt, if not scary, at least alien, wrong, not my area, which was presumably the source of the fear as a child. It was where I didn't belong, and the further I got along it, the stranger it seemed, until I turned the third corner, to the last, short corridor, when I came to a halt, looking along it, but not wanting to walk to the end.

But though I had stepped directly into my memory and my dreams, I was not back in my past, only in a confirmation of the memory of my past. I was walking through my dreams, not my childhood. I remembered, rather than relived. It was hardly an experience at all, just a reiteration of the accuracy of my memory. But that itself was a little surprising. I had expected to find things different from my recollections.

I rode to the fifth floor – the lifts were new, mirrored and carpeted, though still very small – and got out into what might have been exactly the same corridor. I think as a child each floor felt different, naturally, since I knew that different people lived there. Today, as an adult, I didn't know anyone, so all the floors felt the same. The second flat we lived in, on this floor, was directly opposite the lift. I stood and looked at it. No sounds from inside. A blank door. The things that had happened there. Nothing. I walked along the corridor to the next flat but one, and stood outside the door of the Rosens. There were sounds of a radio. Very tempted, but I didn't knock.

I went part of the way down the back stairs listening to my footsteps echo accurately, and then, on the third floor again, pausing a moment in front of number 38, I walked down the front stairs, less mysterious, as ever.

I left Paramount Court feeling a little disappointed, though I had found exactly what I remembered. I had revisited, but only the memory of my past, not the past itself. The past was gone, though the bricks and mortar remained. This is what I had always felt, so I shouldn't have been surprised, but I'd been protected in a way by never having been back inside the flats. Some part of me hoped I might still be wandering around the corridors, that I'd be available to myself in a new kind of way. I was pleased that my memory was accurate, but found there was no getting beyond simply by placing myself *in situ*.

MRS ROSEN (*after a long pause*): Jennifer? Is that Jennifer?

I took my time about using the information I had found in the porter's office. It was a couple of weeks before I looked up the names Rosen and Levine in the phone book and found their numbers, and a while after that before I picked up the phone. I called Mrs Rosen who, according to the directory, did indeed live next door but one to the fifth-floor flat I had lived in. If it was the same woman, Jonathan's mother – could it possibly be? – then she would have been my neighbour.

I introduced myself as Jenny Diski and explained who my parents were and which flat we had lived in. I then reintroduced myself in the silence. 'Jenny Diski – Jenny Simmonds, I used to play with Jonathan. You are Jonathan's mother, aren't you?'

That was when she said 'Jennifer', and I felt an odd wooziness come over me. I almost said no, not recognizing myself by that name. But I had been Jennifer when I was small, though for the life of me I only really remember being Jenny.

I said yes, but felt fraudulent, which was curious because I never really like being called Jenny. *Diski* feels more accurately like me, though it is an entirely invented name to which both Roger-the-Ex and I changed on a whim when we got married. There was a gasp and then a brief silence.

'How are you?'

I was eleven when she had last known me, but what else was there to say?

'I'm well, thank you.'

I explained that I was a writer these days and was thinking about doing a book in part about my mother, that I didn't know anyone who knew us when we were a family at Paramount Court; would it be possible for me to come and talk to her, to get, as it were, an outside view of what went on?

'You and Jonathan were at the same school. Your mother and I took both of you the first day, you were only four. You went in quite happily. She cried when you'd gone. We went for a cup of coffee.'

My mother cried. Lord, she did love me. Then again, she would be on her own when I was at school. Cried for herself, probably. Leave it for later.

'Mrs Levine and Mrs Gold are still here. Do you remember Helen Levine and Marianne Gold, you used to play together? You're a writer you say? You're all right, then?'

'Yes. I'd really like to come and talk to you about my parents.'

There was an awkward pause. I liked the sound of her voice. London Jewish, parents foreign speaking, brought up in the East End. She sounded alert and thoughtful, you could hear her remembering and considering what she remembered.

'Well, we were friends of your mother, of course. But . . . I'm afraid you didn't have a very happy childhood.' This last was said hesitantly, telling me there were things she thought I'd better not know.

'No, it was a bit of a mess, wasn't it?'

'Oh, you remember it, do you? You had a terrible time. I thought you would have forgotten. Well, in that case . . .'

I established that I wanted to know what had gone on from her – a contemporary adult's – point of view, and that I wasn't at all sensitive about what she had to tell me. She seemed encouraged by that, and we arranged a date a few days off when I could come round to tea.

I was thrown by Mrs Rosen's genuine surprise that I recollected my childhood as being less than classically happy. At first I wondered if the idea of false memory syndrome had seeped deeper into the general consciousness than I had supposed. Why would I have blanked out what she seemed to remember? Because I couldn't stand to remember it, would be the post-Freudian supposition. But more likely the source of her surprise was the pre-Freudian notion that children are not really conscious entities. A comforting thought this for parents who can manage it. Odd how the modern notion of repressed memory syndrome fits with this more archaic formulation of childhood. What the pre- and post-Freudians have in common is the desire to believe children suppress

92

unhappiness. Either it washes over them, or it washes under them. Take your choice. Either way, knowing clearly what happened isn't on the cards.

The sound of my parents fighting in our two-roomed flat on the third floor echoed through the corridors of Paramount Court, my father leaving several times, my mother being stretchered away to hospital, the furniture and fittings being confiscated by debt collectors when we were on the fifth floor: these were all public events, but somehow, it was assumed, I wouldn't retain a memory of those things. Adults experience, children don't. Enter Freud, announcing that even pre-conscious infants can experience, but still the idea of suppression held sway. They remember, but don't know they remember. Still, children and their experience are divorced from each other. Either way, parents have an opt-out, in the first case for life, in the second, until their offspring lie down on the psychiatrist's couch. Then the new, paid 'parent' brings it all back to them in vivid feelovision and well, everything's all right again. I recall my mother and father complaining about my firstly nervous and then wayward behaviour, as if what happened between them had nothing to do with me. 'Why are you like this?' they'd demand, outraged and genuinely puzzled that I should be so difficult. 'Oh, you remember, do you?' said Mrs Rosen.

Well, I remembered all sorts of things, and some of them the sort of thing you are supposed to keep hidden from your adult self, but what I lacked was corroboration and background. Neither of my parents told clear stories about themselves, most of the stuff I knew about them (as opposed to what I *knew* happened between them) came from outbursts designed to give pain or pay back a bad deed: 'Now, I'll tell you the truth . . .' The truth was always unpleasant and about the other partner, it always upturned some previous cover story, and it was told as revelation, with the purpose of enlightening me as to the true nature of the monster who was one of my parents. The truth was dangerous, the truth was poison. The phrase 'Now, I'll tell you the truth . . .' made me flinch, knowing something was going to be said that would never be unsaid, and would live inside my head whether I wanted it or not. Neither of my parents, I came to understand, told the truth about themselves, only about each other, and the truth was never something to look forward to. As a result, I think, I've never respected the truth very much. It came and went according to emotions and in the end just told another, different story from the previous story.

The *truth* – she would tell me – was that my father had been in prison when I was very small and my mother had covered up the fact so I wouldn't think less of him. The *truth* – she would announce – was that my father's son by his first marriage had been killed, not, as they had previously told me, getting off a bus on the way home from school and being run over by the one behind, but running out of the house during a fight between his parents and falling under an oncoming bus. The *truth* – she'd declare – was that my father left my mother and I alone till all hours of the night, even when I was ill, because he was carrying on with some woman or other.

The *truth* – the truth that she concealed but now would reveal to me – was that my father did not love me as he said he did, was a bastard and a crook and a coward.

The *truth* – my father would tell me – was that my mother had never had a breakdown when she was carried out of the flat after he left, but had faked it in order to get attention and to make my father return to her. The *truth* – he announced – was that her first husband came back from the war and was grateful to my father for taking my mother off his hands. The *truth* – he said – was that my mother drank, gambled, and had no interest in anything but the spending of money. The *truth* – he disclosed – was that she insisted on being made unconscious when she gave birth to me, that she refused to touch me to change my nappies and that my father had had to do it. The *truth* – he told me – was that my mother had taken my father to court for my custody only as a ploy to get regular alimony and she had offered a deal before the session started whereby he could have me if she could have a fiver a week. The *truth* – he revealed – was that my mother and Pam, the woman my father was living with, made a deal before I went to live with my father at twelve to ensure that she would treat me in such a way that I would be unhappy there and want to return to my mother.

Between his truths about her and her truths about him were their truths about me. Mostly these were to do with me being dangerously like her (he said) or dangerously like him (she said). Mad, bad, evil, heartless, lazy, hard, undisciplined, inadequate, self-centred. Sometimes, like an opera, their rows would rage above my head and then precipitate down, suddenly including me. *And what about you?* I just sat there and listened, I didn't care, I thought it was funny, I was on his side, I was on her side. WHOSE SIDE WAS I ON? Eventually, this question would come up and seem to bring them together. They would both turn to look at me and genuinely expect an answer. Sometimes I played the little judge and said which argument seemed the most just; sometimes I mumbled that I didn't know; sometimes I just stayed shtoom. It didn't matter, all hell would rain down on my head whichever answer I gave or none.

All this was *truth*. Truth, I learned, was up for grabs, entirely dependent on who was doing the telling. Truth was something that happened secretly in the back of people's minds and came out of those minds like exploding sewage when there was enough anger or fear to impel it. Two things I learned from this: be very wary of the truth, and try to keep tabs on what is in the back of your own mind. Keep checking on what is there, don't let it seep into dark corners, loitering unseen until suddenly it jumps out at you. Know what you know. And try and know what others know, keep a check on their dark corners, never mind how ugly or improbable. It's a kind of armour against the rapier words. Never let yourself be surprised.

You are, perhaps, by now a little chronologically confused. It's hardly surprising, my childhood and adolescence were busy times. Sometimes I get confused myself about the order of events during those days. Why shouldn't you? A certain amount of confusion is inevitable, but let me offer a brief chronology.

Between birth and six or seven, I lived with my parents on the third floor of Paramount Court. When I was about six, and money had become a problem, my father left. He had left before, but this was more decisive, apparently. My mother suffered a breakdown, was taken into a mental hospital and I was sent to stay with a foster family for two or three months. My father returned and when my mother was discharged, we moved upstairs to the fifth floor, where I had a room of my own. By now, money was a constant concern. My father left again, this time for good, when I was eleven, towards the end of my time at primary school. He disappeared and sent no money. The bailiffs came, emptied the flat, and we were awaiting eviction when I flipped and refused to go to school. When the social workers arrived to see what had become of me, they got my mother a room in Mornington Crescent, put her on social security, and had me sent to the progressive boarding school in Letchworth.

I was there a term or two, then left and lived with my mother who was working with no great success as a housekeeper in a fancy house in Hampstead Garden Suburb, and I attended a local grammar school. My mother left or was sacked, and we drifted about north London, staying in bed and breakfast places for a while on the remains of her wages. Finally, at twelve, without telling my mother, I got in touch with my father, who in spite of 'disappearing' turned out still to be working where he had been when he lived with us. I ran away, and stayed with him and the woman, Pam, that he lived with until his death. At two points, he and I moved out and lived alone in a flat, once in Bristol, later back in London. Each time, when his current romance failed to work out, we returned to Pam. My mother went to live in Hove. I asked the social workers to send me back to the boarding school. I was nearly thirteen. Eighteen months later, at almost fifteen, I was expelled. Waywardness. My father and Pam had just moved to Banbury, and I lived there for a couple of months, working as a shop assistant (my father, punishing me for getting expelled, wouldn't let me go back to school), until I ran away from them to my mother in Hove. Two days later, I was admitted to my first psychiatric hospital.

Does that help? Perhaps not much.

Three spruce elderly women in their late seventies and early eighties sat in matching white leather armchairs. I, aged forty-eight, shared the sofa with the one remaining husband. All were wearing wedge-heeled mules, and jumpers with bright or gilded patterns. Mrs Levine and Mrs Gold were in neat tracksuit trousers. Mrs Rosen, being the hostess, was a little more formal, in a smart skirt. Their hair was dressed, waved and blown dry and their faces lipsticked and powdered. They were formidably well and at ease with themselves. These eighty-year-olds could have passed for a vigorous sixty. Tea time. Teaspoons tinkling, Mrs Rosen, our hostess, sprang up, demanding I eat more cake – 'You've only had the one slice. You've got to eat, you're too thin' – and topping up the cups. These four, and the two departed husbands, had sat like this, taking tea and chatting since they moved into the flats in 1940. My mother, at times, would have been among them. Newlyweds, young, childless couples, men in the forces, women working and avoiding the bombs. Beginning a life designed to better themselves and provide a good start for the children they were going to have once the war had finished.

'Ninety per cent of these flats were Jewish,' Nathan told me.

'Why?' I wondered. This was Tottenham Court Road, not the East End or Golders Green, why this block of flats?

'The flats had a shelter in the basement. The Jews know how to take care of themselves,' laughed Mrs Rosen. 'And there was the rag trade around Great Portland Street, it was convenient for the tailors.'

And the war? The knowledge that the Nazis were just a few miles away, across the Channel? How did that impinge on their daily life?

'We felt safe here. We were all just twenty, and at that age it didn't bother us. We went to business as usual. To tell you the truth, we didn't really think about it.'

The Jewishness of our neighbours and ourselves was plain during my childhood. There was almost nothing in the way of religious practice in my family, though when I was very young my mother lit candles on Friday nights, and my father would take me to the local synagogue on the last night of Yom Kippur to hear the ram's horn being blown. But our Jewishness was constantly reiterated: by my parents in their everyday conversation – bits of Yiddish from their East End immigrant families; whether famous people in the news were or were not Jewish; in what we ate – fried fish on Fridays, chicken soup with knedleich, bagels, soured cream, lockshen pudding; being Jewish was in the air. It was also evident from the outside world. At school the other kids told me I was not English, but Jewish. Killing Christ was still something – just a few years after the Second World War – I was held responsible for in the playground. Helen Levine, who, oddly, went to a Catholic school nearby the flats, was told to go home and look at her mother's feet by one of the nuns to see if they didn't have demonic hooves. She went to school somewhere else not long after. Nor, being Jewish, could I ever quite fit myself into the English class system. We weren't middle class, not exactly working class; it was *different*. Much easier now to see that we were the children of immigrants. The parallels with second- and third-generation Asian families are now clear to me. My parents' own lack of culture did not mean they had no interest in it for their daughter. Getting on was the thing, in every and any way possible. My parents, in their view, had got on from their impoverished East End beginnings; money was the key. I was to get on further, enabled by their relative wealth, to achieve a good education, a good career and a good marriage.

It was, I think, like this for all the Jewish children in those flats.

As we sipped our tea, the day of my visit, Mrs Rosen, Mrs Levine and Mrs Gold were as comfortable and snappy with each other as any group of people who have known each other, day in, day out for well over fifty years. Mrs Levine spoke less than the others, but began nearly all her comments with, 'Well, of course, I had to go to work, so I wasn't here during the day.' Partly, this was to emphasize that she, unlike the other women, carried on working after she had children, and partly it excused her from knowing very much. There was an incident she recalled, though, that happened on a Thursday afternoon, Mrs Levine's afternoon off. It started the ball rolling.

'Your mother came to my door that afternoon. Somebody was desperately ill, she said, or something like that. I can't remember. She came up and asked me if I'd like to go to church. I said, why would I want to go to church? But she went. To a church in Trafalgar Square.'

Nathan asked, 'Why not a synagogue?'

'I don't know. She had a reason for going to church. It wasn't a religious reason, I don't think. But I don't know any more about it. It was my afternoon off.'

In fact, she took me instead. I stood outside South Africa House waiting, while she disappeared into St Martin-in-the-Field. I hadn't the faintest idea what she was doing and she didn't tell me. I used it as a key scene in my novel, *The Dream*

101

Mistress. I remember it very clearly – even so, it was a jolt to hear it being confirmed by someone else. Confirmed, but not explained.

My mother was a woman whose behaviour was often inexplicable. It's quite possible that she didn't know why she needed to go to a church other than feeling an urgent impulse. God was often on her lips: why had he allowed her mother to die so young; why was he punishing her with my evil father; why didn't he help her? Perhaps she thought she ought to try another god. If the Jewish god didn't work, maybe the Christian one would. Worth a try. My mother's religion was coterminous with her sense of personal injustice: a primitive, minimal belief that someone, somewhere, ought to be looking after her. She was barely educated, she was not cerebral. She responded to pressing emotional needs as an infant responds to its physical wants – instantly, thoughtlessly. I imagine her operating almost entirely unfettered by the rational functions of her forebrain. When she was in pain, she screamed and howled, and hit out; and she was, while I knew her, frequently in emotional pain, suffering a total disappointment at the way her life had gone. She was frightening in her reactions because the most apparently minor setbacks seemed to her catastrophic and she responded appropriately. Her bitterness and her lack of control caused me anxiety and worse, but I don't think it was done with deliberate malice. I don't believe she thought enough about what she did for malice consciously to be present. She hit out, gave full rein to her feelings, and couldn't do otherwise. She was sad, rather than bad, and, I think, genuinely baffled by the way life was out of her control. She did not, for reasons of her own emotionally deprived upbringing, have enough insight to be considered responsible for the results of her behaviour. It leaves me little room for anger towards her personally. Living with her, day by day, was like skating on newly formed ice. It constantly shattered, every day, but there was no alternative, no other place to go. No room for anger, but no room for affection either. She often told me, yelled at me, that everyone needed their mother. That I would need her one day, when she wouldn't be there and then I'd realize . . . I was certainly not without needs, but whatever it was I needed, it wasn't her, even if she was my mother. I cannot recall a moment in my life when I have wished she was there. Thinking about her as my mother, I can only manage a shrug, a sense of random misfortune that I was in the charge of a woman with the emotional capacity of a small child. Bad, sad luck; human child-rearing arrangements are a crap shoot. You might as well be enraged at the ice for being too fragile to hold your weight.

Mrs Gold clearly didn't like to be overlooked and was not going to be outdone by the recollections of Mrs Levine.

'I can tell you something else,' she jumped in eagerly. 'Your father rented a room in Albany Street. You didn't know that, did you? He was a charmer. But he was a confidence man.'

Mrs Levine looked a little alarmed. 'Doesn't she mind?' she asked Mrs Rosen, meaning me.

'No,' explained Mrs Rosen, 'she wants to know. She said so.'

103

'Well, Jimmy was a confidence man,' Mrs Gold continued. 'He rented this room in Albany Street, on top of the woman who made the curtains, what was her name?'

A small flutter of reminiscence overcame the three women.

'Oh, I know,' said Mrs Levine, 'Claire, Stella . . .'

'Anyway,' said Mrs Gold. 'He did a lot of confidence tricks in this place. He had money sent to him. He wrote letters out. He used the room as a postage address. And the woman became a very wealthy woman, she had a curtain place in Vivian Avenue.'

'I had her here to estimate for curtains,' Mrs Rosen remembered.

'That's right. And Jimmy was named as a correspondent while he was living in Paramount Court.'

Whether he was named as correspondent to the curtain woman's divorce, or one of the women from whom he extorted money in return for romance, was not made clear. The recollections were all like this: sharp and hazy simultaneously. The old women remembered what they remembered, but they claimed not to know the details because they hadn't asked questions, wouldn't have interfered in another family's business. So they knew he had a room in Albany Street and that he was a professional con man, but they didn't know exactly what kind of activities he got up to, and had no idea why he was imprisoned, even though to have a family in the flats with the father in prison must have been remarkable at the time.

I had known my father was something of a villain in a black-marketeering, womanizing sort of way. I hadn't known that he was a con artist by profession, with an office and everything. This was, if not entirely new information, a shift of emphasis.

'Was he caught?' I asked.

'I remember he was in prison, for what reason I cannot tell you, but all I know is it was whispered behind your mother's back that it was through these letters. You would have been tiny, about three. Then soon after that, this tragedy happened.' Mrs Gold was well into her stride. 'Maybe it was before he went to prison, because he knew he was going to be caught. Or after. I don't remember, but he came into our shop in Great Portland Street one morning and asked my husband to go horse racing with him. I said, why does he suddenly want to go horse racing with you, coming round out of the blue, on a working day? My husband told him he couldn't leave the shop. Then he went to Epping Forest, but he was saved.'

'Pardon,' I said.

'He was found in the car in Epping Forest, with the exhaust pipe. You know?'

'Of course, that wasn't the only time,' Mrs Rosen added. 'He tried to do it again. When you were at St David's, your first school. I went down to see if you were going to school that day and your mother was in a bit of a state. You'd gone to Southend or somewhere with Sally Leigh, rest her soul. It was a very, very hot day. And you came back.'

'It was very hot in the sun, wasn't it?' chirped Mrs Gold.

'And the next day, also in the car, the exhaust. He tried again. I don't know where.'

I remember one occasion when a policeman arrived at the flat and told my mother that my father had been found in his car with a pipe from the exhaust leading through the window. I hadn't known he'd made a habit of it.

On an impulse I asked, 'Did my mother try to commit suicide, ever?'

'Not that I know of,' said kindly Mrs Rosen, rather quickly.

'I think she did,' corrected Mrs Gold. 'She did. An overdose. How old were you then? Five, I think.'

I'm washing down this family history of social crime and multiple suiciding with my second cup of tea. Still, Mrs Rosen wishes I would have another piece of cake. But I've got a small appetite.

While, rather contemptuously, I am unable to be angry at my mother's inadequacy, on the grounds that she knew no better, I have always had a healthy anger about my father. He came from a poor but close family. He was not uneducated. He was a bright boy and won a scholarship to an East End Foundation School. According to him – not a reliable source – he began an undergraduate course at Cambridge, but gave it up in the second term in order to earn money. Whether this was true or not, he prided himself on his cleverness. That was what he and I had in common; what sidelined my mother. We were clever, she wasn't. 'Never mind,' he would say when she was sulking or shouting, 'Mummy doesn't understand.' He did not have her excuse for his behaviour. But it was beginning to look as if they were more similar than I had imagined. That her hysteria was matched by his and that intellectual capacity and a decent education were no proof against emotional unreliability. Two infants for parents. A well-matched pair. Double bad luck.

'Do you know why he tried to kill himself?' I asked. Somehow my mother's suicide attempts didn't need a motive.

'I think it was frustration,' suggested Mrs Rosen.

'No, it was all to do with those letters he was sending.'

'And gambling. He took a chance on everything, he loved gambling.'

'He was desperate.'

'Desperate.'

'He despaired.'

'So sad, so sad.'

'Very sad.'

'Terrible. Her mother was a pretty little woman, that I do remember. She had a nice face.'

'A nice smile.'

'And very smart before she, you know . . . And you had the most wonderful clothes before . . .'

'He had a head of silver hair,' remembered Mrs Gold. 'He was so handsome. And charming.'

'Absolutely charming. A perfect gentleman.'

'He did have something about him,' cooed Mrs Gold.

The three old ladies lost themselves in a rhapsody to the charms of my father.

'He was such a gentleman,' recalled Mrs Levine. 'He was going to get my Anthony into the City of London school. He was very friendly with the Lord Mayor of London. He said to my husband, I will get your son into the City of London. And Jimmy, God rest his soul, came up, sat down, and wrote this letter. We had a letter . . . I must look and see if I can find it . . .'

'Do you think my father perhaps made promises he couldn't keep?' I wondered.

'Well, it was in black and white. To us, my husband and I, it seemed genuine. Absolutely genuine. He had a way with him. He was a charmer.'

'Yes, I remember,' I said. 'But I don't think he was the most straightforward person. Did he get Anthony into the City of London?'

'Well, he had gone by then, but I'm sure, if he'd been there . . . I'm sure it was genuine.'

'He had a wonderful way.'

'A very handsome man. A ladies' man.'

'And so smart. Beautifully spoken, so dapper.'

'Where did your mother find him?' wondered Mrs Gold jarringly, a little rasp in her voice.

'He could talk anybody into anything. He had that personality. The way he spoke, you had to listen to him.'

'Anybody would have been taken in,' Nathan Rosen added quietly.

'He had personality, didn't he? As soon as you spoke to him you felt you'd known him all your life.'

'He was very generous. Always the first to put his hand in his pocket. You had to love him.'

'Maybe too much,' said Nathan, quietly again, bringing the song to an end.

After a quiet moment Mrs Rosen asked hesitantly, lowering her voice, 'Tell me, did he ever abuse you, your father?'

This was jolting, coming in this room of respectable, elderly people, for whom discretion and decency were keys to contentment. Extraordinary that the delicately thoughtful Mrs Rosen could have voiced this thought, amid the china ornaments and professionally posed photographs in her immaculate living room. In the hush that awaited my answer, I realized fully how the word 'abuse' has become such a pervasive modern euphemism, suggestive yet unclear, a declaration of something shocking without *saying* anything shocking. As effective as a Victorian covering for table legs, concealing but pointing to the thrillingly vulgar, the word *incest* tickling the back of the throat without being spoken. It felt like a trick question, one that needed careful definition; this company would not want too frank an answer.

What flashed into my mind as I considered what to say next, were those nights, many of them, when my naked mother (both my parents slept naked) would enter my room in the fifth-floor flat, one door down from where I now sat taking tea, and shake me awake telling me I had to go and sleep with my father because she wasn't going to sleep in the same bed as him. I would stumble out of bed and, as she climbed into mine, go into my parents' bedroom, and clamber into the big double bed in which my father lay. He would put his arms around me and hold me against his hairy chest, rocking me for, I suppose, both our comfort. And pleasure. Certainly mine, I relished the feel and smell of his warm body, as I nuzzled into his hairy chest, and squeezed myself tight up against his beating heart. I adored being held in his arms and feeling his big hands stroking me. Stroking me where? Everywhere, I think. I took in his physical affection like draughts of delicious drink. I don't ever recall feeling anything but safe and loved in this private midnight comforting.

There was a game both my parents used to play when I was small on the occasions when they were in accord. Usually after an evening bath, I would dry myself in the living room and then run naked between them as each, on opposite sides of the room, reached out for my vagina and tried to tickle it. When they caught me, their fingers at my vulva, I would squeal and shriek and wriggle with the equivocal agony tickling engenders, and the game would go on until I was exhausted and they were weak with laughter. It was my family's way of having a good time, and there were so few good times that these occasions have a golden haze over them as I recollect them. Looking back, it's clear to what extent I was a conduit between them, in good times and bad, a lightning rod for their excitement and their misery. Whatever feelings they wanted to express, and could barely articulate, were channelled through me. When they bounced me back and forth between them, grabbing for my sex, they were, I imagine, communicating with each other as best they might. But those dark nights in bed with my father felt like a private exchange between me and him. They weren't, of course; it was just a child's mis-reading of herself as the centre of the universe. I was sent to sleep with my father by my mother, and while, as a child, I supposed that they had had another argument in bed, what was more likely was my mother's (or my father's) sexual refusal, and her insistence that I take her place. The same pattern as the living room game.

It was only later with the arrival of a sense of sexual privacy when I was fourteen that I responded in what might now be considered an appropriate way. I had run away from my father and Pam in Banbury, and gone to my mother, who was living in a single room in Hove. On the night of my arrival, I was curled up facing away from her, when she climbed under the covers of the small bed we had to share. I wasn't asleep, but she thought I was. She slipped a hand around my pelvis and down between my legs, and began to caress me. I was mortified.

'Don't do that,' I snapped.

'It's all right,' she said. 'You're my little girl. My baby. There's nothing wrong with your mummy touching her little baby.'

'Stop it,' I shouted, horribly embarrassed, and pulled away from her. With a tut of irritation, she turned her back in a familiar sulk. I didn't sleep that night. We argued all the next day about where I would live, and in the evening I swallowed a handful of Nembutal I found in her drawer. By the following day, I was an inmate in the Hove psychiatric hospital, and my mother and father would meet each other for the first time for years over my hospital bed, each shouting at me, 'How could you do this to me?' as I lay between them and pulled the covers over my head and began to scream.

'Do you mean, did he hit me?' I asked Mrs Rosen, cautiously.

'Yes,' she said, looking sympathetic. 'I know he hit your mother. Did he ever lift his hand to you?'

'They both smacked me sometimes. They would get into rages and slap my face, but it wasn't a big thing. Nothing special,' I assured her.

Warm-hearted Mrs Rosen looked genuinely relieved.

There are no photographs of me or my mother before I was eleven. After my father left for the last time – the money had long run out, and we were on the point of being evicted from Paramount Court – my mother took the laundry box full of old photos and the blue album (of my parents before I was born, of me from birth until the present) and handed them to Bill the Stoker. He worked in the boiler-room in the bowels of the building, stoking the fires that kept the centralized central heating pumping through the pipes. Sometimes, I would visit Bill and watch him at work. For some reason, my mother entrusted our photographs to him, telling him she would collect them when she had sorted something out.

There wasn't much else; the furniture, carpets, my books and toys had gone when the bailiffs took them away in lieu of unpaid bills, and we had been living on potatoes fried in stored chicken fat for weeks. My mother did not want the other people in the flats, the Rosens, Golds and Levines to know of our shameful predicament. We walked shoeless on the bare boards in case the downstairs neighbours guessed we were carpetless and I was instructed to behave as normal if I met any of them in the corridors and the streets, and I had to keep away from the other children. All that was left in the way of memorabilia were the laundry box of photos I used to lie on the floor and pore over, and a blue leather-bound volume of photographs devoted to me from birth onwards. There had been another album, a maroon one, with photos of my father's dead son, Stanley, from his first marriage, stacked on top of mine. My father took that one with him when he left.

Some years later, when I was sixteen and working nearby in an office in Goodge Street, I summoned up the courage to call the porter's lodge at Paramount Court – though with little hope, the five years since the photos were deposited with Bill seemed like aeons to me. I said who I was, and the porter said, in a significant voice, that yes, he remembered the family. Of course, anyone would who was still working there. But Bill the Stoker was long gone. He didn't know where and he didn't know anything about any photographs. Probably, he said without malice, Bill had burned them when no one came to claim them. Probably he did. They would have meant nothing to him.

I mourned, and still mourn, the loss of those photos. I recall glamorous pictures of my mother and father during the war, their good time, in evening dress in night-clubs. Like the movies. One photo showed my mother sitting in shorts on some steps by a beach, and standing beside her, smiling, was

Douglas Fairbanks Jnr, who, my mother explained, was a film star with whom she had made friends while holidaying during the fat years in the south of France. There was something about the way she said this that suggested they might have been quite close, but perhaps her wistfulness was merely the wishful thinking of a disappointed woman. There were photographs of me as an infant, in party frocks, white socks and gloves, of me at the zoo, skating, dancing – all the usual childhood photos, but I can't remember them with any clarity. They were much, I suppose, like the photos of Chloe developing from babyhood to young womanhood that fill several albums, and cover the hall wall of my flat. Nearly all of these photos were taken by her father who is keen on photography. I hardly ever use a camera, don't even own one, but I was scrupulous about getting copies of photos of Chloe from Roger, and sticking the pictures in the albums until Chloe took over the task herself. There has always been some comfort in the thought that there are two sets of photos of Chloe's life, one at her father's house, one here. One of the benefits of amicable separation. A fail-safe device against accidental loss. Whatever might have happened to Jennifer, there is no photographic evidence for it, only those unreliable memory snapshots that must do service for the past.

Three days turned out to be long enough for institutional regularity to set in. By day two we were in a floating boarding school or hospital: naturally, it was the hospital metaphor I most inclined towards. Happily for my fantasy, I developed a rolling, murky headache that I carried about with me for twenty-four hours. The Extra Strong Anadin I'd brought in a jumbo-sized tub, wouldn't touch it. Butch told me that a headache is what some people get instead of nausea at sea, and suggested I see the ship's doctor. I was quite taken with seeing someone who wore a white coat.

The Russian doctor was as small and round and hirsute as a bearded indiarubber ball. When he grinned, which he did a lot instead of talking, since he had no English, his mouth blazed like the risen sun with the gleam of a quantity of gold teeth. He had more than any of the crew, though all the Russians flashed golden beams from at least one or two canines. The doctor was originally a dentist, so perhaps this explained why he had the most. It seemed to be a sign of status among the crew, possibly among Russians in general, to have as many gold teeth as you could afford, like tennis players and gold necklaces, I suppose. I confess that my first

thought was that it was the height of folly for people to wear
their gold in their mouth. Best to keep it detached from the
body, where it can be taken without physical harm, so history
and modern urban life tell me. But the evident pleasure the
small round doctor got from flashing his gilded choppers
eventually charmed away my fear for him.

He pointed with a dazzling smile to his stomach, which
was not distinguishable from his chest or even his thighs
except by its general position. I pointed to my head, and
placed my palm over it, Victorian-lady-in-distress style. He
pointed again to his stomach and shook his head. I shook mine
back. He nodded and looked happy at the efficiency of our
communication, pulling from his white doctor's jacket a silver
card with five large pills embedded in it. They were white
with erratic splodges of green, like porcelain teeth that have
just eaten spinach. He held up one finger and then, putting it
away, a whole handful of fingers. I was either to take all five at
one go, or one every five hours. He confirmed the latter by
pointing to his watch, almost hidden in the black undergrowth
of hair on his wrist, and then showing me five fingers again. I
smiled my understanding; he smiled back his pleasure at my
understanding and said something quite substantial in Russian
to which I nodded and said 'Thank you' (or rather 'spa-see-ba'
as suggested on the sheet of twelve basic Russian phrases
thoughtfully placed in the cabin), because I was sure he was
telling me that once I had taken his tablets I would feel perfectly fine again. Only after he left did it occur to me that he
might have been telling me on no account to eat tuna fish or

lemon soufflé while taking them. The spinach tablets worked a treat, after just three my headache vanished like a bad memory is supposed to, and I was a fit and happy cruiser once again.

The expedition crew had high anxiety about the long, landless sea journey. Like flight attendants in aeroplanes they did their best to keep the passengers from the dangerous effects of boredom. Meals, lectures, organized card championships, videos filled the hours, as if sixty empty minutes might have had us climbing the walls, muttering dissatisfactions, fomenting mutiny. I knew I had to play the timetable game, or seem aloof and unfriendly – not a good idea on a small ship I would have to be on for two weeks.

At breakfast I sat cheerily opposite Big Jim and his mountain of five sausages, several fried eggs and two or three blueberry muffins teetering on the edge of his plate.

'Hi, how ya doing?' he asked, not looking up from his knife and fork. 'Sea sick? Lots of people are.'

Sea sickness was not Big Jim's problem. I told him I'd had a headache in lieu of sea sickness but the fine Russian doctor cured me.

'Well, if you need any drugs, just come to me. I'm a walking pharmacy. Never go away without a complete medicine chest. Tranquillizers, antibiotics, codeine – you need it, I got it.'

I thanked him, genuinely comforted by the prospect of Big Jim's bag of tricks.

Obediently, I attended Jerry's lecture on 'Life at Sea: Is it for the Birds?' My heart, already at half mast, sank as he arrived with a replica of a dead white bird strung around his neck. He related for us the story of the Ancient Mariner which, it seemed, was written by someone called Samuel Taylor *Coolridge* – a presidential poet, doubtless. The eyes of the British contingent began to slide around in their sockets. The albatross in question would have been the Wandering Albatross, seen only in these parts, a huge bird, pure white, which stays on the wing for all its life, except for landing once a year in order to mate. Manny interrupted several times to make desperate jokes about Albert Ross. Jerry, a bewhiskered Alaskan not gifted with Manny's or anyone else's sense of humour, failed to see the point and carried on showing his slides of petrels – snowy, giant, white-chinned, Cape and Snow, skuas – the sky pirates, brown and South Polar, and albatrosses aplenty – royal, black-browed, light-mantled, grey-headed and wandering. Not one of these would I be able to recognize when I stood at the back of the ship watching *birds*, big ones and small ones, light ones and dark ones, pretty ones and dull ones, following in our wake.

The birders were a very special group, and probably the expedition crew's sole delight – none of them needed entertaining. They were up (as I was, once or twice) at five in the morning, fully weather-proofed, nothing but eyes visible, standing in bunches at the stern, or at either side of the bridge, scanning the skies with their alarmingly huge binoculars. The BA purser was a bit of a loner, often seen at the side of the ship, still in his suit and city shoes (which caused him immense difficulty on the wet deck) but well parkaed up and standing in one position for hours against the railing waiting for the birds to fly into view. When I tried to focus my (as I thought) quite expensive enough binoculars on some moving speck I failed to see anything – birds move too fast. No sooner had I caught a feather in my view than it disappeared and I had to wiggle around trying to find it and always failing. A Canadian birder took one eye from the sky to explain briefly to me that my equipment wouldn't do. 'No point in looking through anything you've spent less than $1,000 dollars on.' I hadn't spent $1,000, so I stopped, and found I could follow the birds' flight quite adequately with just my spectacles. I could even see that one of the birds had a black semicircle over its eye. 'Aha,' I cried, triumphant, 'A black-browed albatross!' It was. My honour was satisfied and I returned to looking at generic flying creatures swoop, swerve and skim over the water.

None of the birders took photographs, they only looked in order to identify. Then they'd drop their binoculars on to their chest and tick off their sighting on a printed grid. Date, time, number of birds seen. Later, during meals, they'd all sit together – even the BA purser – to share their sightings, huddled close, consulting each other's lists and querying doubtful identifications. We had been issued with our groupings for the landings – there were between seven and nine passengers to each Zodiac. The birders complained that they were scattered about on the Zodiacs, and the list had to be redone so that all of them could occupy the same boat. They became the butt of the rest of the ship. The school swots.

The first full day at sea, the sun came out for long periods and it felt incredibly warm. Climbing up to the small topmost deck, I saw a pair of naked legs sticking out from behind a weather tower. One of the Russian sailors lay splayed out in his bathing trunks on a towel, glistening from tanning lotion. I crept away not wanting to disturb his R and R. The following day was quite different, much colder, and though the sea was calm with just a few whitecaps dancing on the surface, there was a biting, dry, icy edge to the air. We were 54 degrees South, past the Roaring Forties and into the Furious Fifties, 450 miles still from South Georgia where we would land the next morning.

I chose this particular trip precisely because there was to be a landing in South Georgia, and I was not alone. There were four others, at least, for whom the name of South Georgia resonated with wonder. The cause was the astonishing journey of Ernest Shackleton in 1914 on the *Endurance* expedition. Though we hadn't demanded a Zodiac to ourselves, we had located each other and a small, informal Shackleton fan club had formed.

I didn't plan this journey as a pilgrimage of any kind, just a hopeful voyage into whiteness. My motives were as indistinct as the landscape I was wishing to travel to. There was simply an irrational desire to be at the bottom of the world in a land of ice and snow. I wanted to write *white* and shades of white, though even this didn't necessarily require me to go to such lengths. Wanting to write *green*, I wrote a novel about a rainforest without feeling the need to go anywhere as sweaty and insect-ridden as an actual jungle. A quick trip to Kew and a few books did the trick. So what it came down to was that I wanted to *be* there, in a white, empty, unpeopled, silent landscape. Perhaps I urgently wanted to be on the moon, but that was marginally more difficult to arrange.

The search for roots is a legitimate excuse for travel these days, but I'm a middle-aged Jewish Londoner, and there was not much chance of finding the source of these aspects of myself in the South Polar regions. Nor would the other travellers' excuse for travelling wash: the search for alternative ways of life. Human life is absent in Antarctica except for a handful of base camp personnel, and the lifestyles of non-human forms such as the penguin and wandering albatross hardly offer an improvement on even the most dismal of societies. Nor was I a scientist, aching to add to the sum total of human knowledge. To tell the truth, I do not feel very exercised about the hole in the ozone layer, though I made sure to cover myself with the right SPF when bathing in the sun. What's more, I hate being cold. My central heating is always turned up several degrees too high for visitors, and I've taken to caching cashmere sweaters so that, come my impoverished old age, at least I won't feel the cold.

And I had no particular interest in tales of exploration and derring-do. I'd never even got around to reading *Swallows and Amazons* as a child, so deeply uninterested was I in boats and adventure. Robert Falcon Scott represented some telling flaw in the English character, I knew, though I hadn't been interested enough to find out exactly why. Before I decided to go to

121

Antarctica and began to read up on the subject, I had barely heard of Shackleton. I didn't even associate him with the south – for all I was aware he might have sailed the Pacific and discovered the Trobriand Islands.

When I finally settled down before my trip to read Cherry-Garrard's *The Worst Journey in the World* and *South*, Shackleton's account of the *Endurance* voyage, I was immediately lost in wonder. Apsley Cherry-Garrard's story of Scott's last expedition is as wracking a tale as any monumental fiction. It might have been written with a pen dipped in tears, for all Cherry-Garrard's pride at what was undoubtedly great bravery and camaraderie. For science, he, along with Wilson and Bowers, spent five weeks fighting through the blizzards of Antarctic winter night in temperatures of 70 below freezing in order to collect Emperor penguin eggs so that Wilson could use the embryos to prove that penguins were interstitial between birds and reptiles. He was wrong, but that wasn't the point. The point was that when things were at their worst, when the three men had had their tent ripped from over them by a monstrous wind and were buried for many hours in the snow, knowing they couldn't survive the exposure, they sang songs, remembered to say 'please' and 'thank you' and no one uttered a single profanity. The otherness of Scott's Antarctica is not really the alien landscape and climate of the far south, but the workings of the minds and mores of those men who lived no further back than my grandfather's generation.

And yet, there are hints in even the utterly loyal Cherry-Garrard's memoirs that beyond the heroics and physical and

122

mental fortitude, something was amiss. His description of Scott is a wonder of suppressed equivocation:

Temperamentally he was a weak man, and might very easily have been an irritable autocrat. As it was he had moods and depressions which might last for weeks . . . He cried more easily than any man I have ever known . . . It would be stupid to say that he had all the virtues: he had, for instance, little sense of humour, and he was a bad judge of men . . . And notwithstanding the immense fits of depression which attacked him, Scott was the strongest combination of a strong mind in a strong body that I have ever known. And this because he was so weak! Naturally so peevish, highly strung, irritable, depressed and moody. Practically such a conquest of himself, such vitality, such push and determination and withal in himself such personal and magnetic charm . . . He will go down to history as the Englishman who conquered the South Pole and who died as fine a death as any man has had the honour to die. His triumphs are many – but the Pole was not by any means the greatest of them. Surely the greatest was that by which he conquered his weaker self and became the strong leader whom we went to follow and came to love.

All this was hushed up during the aftermath when the First World War needed English heroes. Now it is accepted that the deaths were unnecessary, arising from a combination of pointless obstinacy and incompetence. These days there are very few of us who feel the world is well lost for a penguin's egg, or that it is an honour to die any kind of death. Oddly enough, it seems that Captain Oates didn't either. Though he is famous for leaving the tent to walk to his death in the snow, making the great sacrifice of his life for the others, the fact is that had he done so just one or two days earlier, there would have been enough supplies for the other three men to get through to the depot just a few miles from where they died. Scott grumbled considerably that Oates was leaving his leave-taking so long. Oates, it seems, understandably to a modern way of thinking, did not want to die a fine death and chose to live until no other option but death was possible. Somehow it makes more sense of what happened, and more decent sense, than the official story.

Brooding seven years later over the deaths of the polar party, Scott, Wilson, Oates, Bowers and Evans, Cherry-Garrard concludes, 'I now see very plainly that though we achieved a first-rate tragedy, which will never be forgotten just because it was a tragedy, tragedy was not our business.'

Shackleton was certainly not in the tragedy business. His most extraordinary adventure was undertaken in order to rescue twenty-two stranded comrades and in all his expeditions not a single life was lost. Scott hated him. Shackleton wasn't Navy, he wasn't a gentleman, he hustled and schemed for money, he wasn't much interested in science, he wanted to reach the pole because he needed the money the fame would bring him. A bit of a chancer. A charmer.

The journey to South Georgia, recounted in *South*, leaves you befuddled. The plan to make a trans-Antarctic crossing was a failure long before they got to Antarctica. The ship, the *Endurance*, was beset in the pack-ice. They lived on or beside the ship through the long winter until it was finally crushed by the ice, then they camped on an ice floe hoping to drift north towards land. For eight months they lived on floating ice which melted around them as the summer came. When the floe was reduced to just fifty feet across they took to three whaling boats and made a five-day journey to Elephant Island, an uninhabited rock in the South Shetlands. With no possibility of rescue – no one knew what had happened to them or where they were – Shackleton and five others of the crew took to a twenty-two-foot open boat and made the 800-mile journey through the world's most storm-ridden ocean to South Georgia to get help. It took sixteen days to reach South Georgia, but they landed on the wrong, uninhabited side of the island. Shackleton, Worsley and Crean set off to cross the mountains to get to the whaling stations on the other side. No crossing had ever been made before of the island which is described as 'a saw-tooth thrust through the tortured upheaval of mountain and glacier that falls in chaos to the northern sea'. The three men crossed it without a sleeping bag between them, not stopping to sleep – they would have died of exposure – not having the faintest idea of what route to take. Since then only a properly equipped mountaineering team has made the crossing just once. After several tries, the soldiers of the British Army stationed there gave up. The men on Elephant

Island were rescued. Not one of Shackleton's crew died, not even the finest of deaths.

The 800 miles we travelled from Ushuaia to South Georgia was almost the same distance as Shackleton's journey from Elephant Island. I spared him a thought or two as I rocked blissfully in my bunk.

John from Phoenix was the most ardent member of our Shackleton Appreciation Society. He was a professor of engineering who was quite in love with our hero. He brought a treasure with him: a videotape of Frank Hurley's original film taken on the *Endurance* expedition. Phoenix John and James Ross (delightfully named but unrelated to the polar explorer) were people I'd only seen in the movies. Both John and James were invariably played by James Stewart, in those movies where through decency and right values he just manages to hold together a world sent mad by greed and corruption. Phoenix John was in his mid-fifties. James, in his late seventies, a big bearish man who wore chequered lumberjack shirts, was also an engineer, though of a different kind to John. His face expressed real pain when he recalled the dark days of Richard Nixon and the eulogies that were heaped on him at his death. He and John were both democrats in some large, humane way that was intended I suspect when the Constitution was written. They were John Waynes without the killer instinct, as romantic about what America means and as disappointed at what it had failed to live up to as any Capra hero. They both read voraciously, loved old movies and relished talk. They were gentle, cultured men who also had that darker aspect that lurked in James

126

Stewart, some unachieved longing, a reticence that, certainly in John, and probably in James, would make them at times moody and reserved, not easy men to live with perhaps. There was an isolated part in each of them that you suspected was utterly unavailable to anyone. John had brought a small dictating machine with him and could be seen at all hours wandering the deck on his own, murmuring surreptitiously into his cupped hand. 'Shackleton's Spy' was how I thought of him.

I saw James lose his good-humoured smile one lunchtime as he and I found ourselves sitting with the Roths. Manny was at his most vocal; something about James egged him on to extremes as he announced that the Indians living off welfare should be forcibly sterilized, that all non-Americans should be denied entry into the States, and that welfare should be abolished for everyone since his family had made their own way through poverty. James's face darkened dangerously, and very quietly, and with a rather alarming control he talked about the Constitution, human rights and America's history of taking in refugees. Manny's voice simply rose higher and his opinions became increasingly loathsome, while Emily backed him up. They were people whose discontent had poisoned the world for them. Wherever they were, they were in strife with those around them, even in Israel.

'Why do you stay in Santa Fe if the people who live there upset you so much?' I asked.

'Ach,' said Emily, her mouth twisting in disgust. 'What's the point of going somewhere else? We've tried everywhere. It would be the same.'

That was almost certainly true. It was as if they were contaminated with their own hatred. It would cling to them wherever they went. Arguing with Manny was playing his game. You might as well argue with the rules of Monopoly. Afterwards, James apologized to me for losing his temper. I said that I thought he had controlled himself remarkably, and how disturbing it was that such opinions shake one so badly, move one so close to wishing to behave violently oneself, but he shook his head. He was apologizing for his feelings, for his warranted but useless inner anger and disgust at what Manny was saying.

Our fellow Shackleton fans were an English couple, taken straight from central casting. Peter and Margaret were well into their seventies and as British as spotted dick. He was in the foreign office, had a neat moustache and spoke with a booming, plummy voice. Margaret was his mirror image, in sensible tweed skirts and twin sets. Both of them talked lovingly and knowledgeably about Shackleton's achievements, and neither seemed other than jolly surprised and amused when one of the women in the crew stepped out in front of them in the corridor from the sauna, stark naked, and rushed leaping into the plunge pool on the upper deck.

'"I say," I said,' related Margaret with a peal of high-pitched, well-bred laughter, '"that woman hasn't got a stitch of clothing on." "Mmm," said Peter, "nor she has, old girl."'

The Ur-American John and James were delighted by the Ur-British Margaret and Peter; they were like characters from their English novel-reading come to life. Both of them were very partial to some imaginary England where decency, they believed, was born and still lives. They saw the decade of Margaret Thatcher as an aberration and were rather apologetic about it, as if, in some way, it was the fault of America. I generously absolved them from responsibility – after all, they had to put up with Reagan, and they nodded sorrowfully.

But being from Britain with a boatload of American citizens was beginning to be a nuisance. The Americans drooled over my accent and on meeting me reminisced about an England they had visited one summer, or possibly had just seen on US television in the form of the *Benny Hill Show*, *Monty Python*, *Upstairs Downstairs* and *Fawlty Towers*. Us Brits drank tea, never coffee; we couldn't cook; it always rains (and as if that weren't enough, the sun never shines); we spend our spare time participating in royal ceremonies; we are economically impoverished and technologically deprived, emotionally buttoned up, but on the plus side we are invariably classically educated and our cultural heritage ('That wonderful National Portrait Gallery of yours . . .') is second to none. People kept informing me of these facts, as if they were true and, if they were true, as if I wouldn't know them. My smile got increasingly brittle.

It positively fell off my face as the afternoon's lecture on the history of whaling got under way, in preparation for our first stop on South Georgia. Tessa was married to Jerry, the Bird Man, and was a skinny, brisk, very outdoorsy Alaskan. She was a thoroughly modern young woman with correct attitudes, who related the dirty history of whaling with all the self-righteous disgust a cosy conscience could muster. She was certainly Jerry's intellectual superior, with a greater command of her subject, but they were, unfortunately, well matched in the sense of humour, or lack of it, department.

South Georgia's only inhabited place, Grytviken, was a whaling station from 1904 to 1965. It has been preserved after a fashion as a museum of whaling and as the site where Shackleton was buried after he died of a heart attack en route to his next Antarctic expedition. These days, of course, we love whales, we think differently and know better about our planet than in the past. I find this 'knowing better' maddeningly smug. As Tessa ran through the details of whaling, the methods of catching, the stripping of blubber, the rendering down and final uses for every possible bit of the whale's body, the audience, my fellow travellers, hissed and clicked their tongues, shook their heads, and covered their eyes as slides flashed on to the screen showing dead whales being butchered. There were actually boos at the sight, and Tessa, telling the story with tight-lipped frankness, waited for the reaction like a comedian pausing for a laugh. There was an especially long silence followed by a murderous murmur, after she told us about the use of whale bones for corsets and other fripperies, and ambergris for fixing perfumes. After the history we got the statistics: how many whales were killed (in Grytviken 54,100 during its active period); how many, or rather how few were left – the slim chances of the most decimated species ever recovering. Further boos and hisses. The tongues tch-tched furiously. Then the finale, pictures of whales gloriously

130

breaching, blowing, diving, swimming with their young, and to cap it all, the eerie song of the humpback from a tape recorder. The sounds of disapproval changed instantly to oohs and ahhs of love for nature at its grandest and most natural.

I like a whale as much as the next person. I'm entirely in favour of animals as well as people being let alone if at all possible. I do not like our ravening *Homo sapiens* way with the world, though of course our *Homo sapiens* way is only more effective ravening than other species can manage. But we had there a boatload of rich folk booing at their wicked forebears for killing something dramatically large. No one mentioned the cruelty of fishing for cod. We were people who could afford to buy free-range chickens so that their brief lives will be a little more comfortable than their battery cousins that only the poor can afford. Most of the commerce in whale products had been in oil, used for lighting and heating before paraffin became available. We no longer need whale bones for our underwear or for any of the things which plastic makes far better. Take away our electricity and petroleum by-products and we would be in the dark and much inconvenienced. The self-righteousness of those who could afford to do without whale products, who had the time and technology to appreciate the beauty of whales in a state of nature, and who had benefited from the wealth of previous unreconstructed commerce, rendered me sullen. This was not respect for life, but sentimentality and thoughtless superiority over people in the past, on whom we had depended to get where we were today. The crowd in the lecture hall looked a lot uglier to me than the long-dead men in the slides, stripping whale blubber with their flensing knives, much less considerate of the creature than Melville's whalemen who had risked their lives to make a living. Whales are still being hunted, despite international whaling commission bans, and their only use is for unnecessarily exotic foodstuffs to titillate the tired palates of the wealthy and their pets. This was booed too, but then it was the Japanese, not the Americans, who were committing the atrocity, and there were no Japanese in the audience. Disapproval always depends on other people – dead people, foreigners – doing the unacceptable action.

I quit the lecture room and stood looking at the sea, which was turquoise like no turquoise I had ever seen. An iridescent, sparkling, blue-tinged green, with white frills dancing on the surface. The clouds were fat and fluffy in a cerulean sky. This was the wild and turbulent South Atlantic? Perhaps the hole in the ozone layer... but I left that disapproval for another day while I rejoiced in the balmy, colour-bright seascape.

John's video of the surviving film taken by Hurley of the *Endurance* expedition was shown the evening before we landed at South Georgia. The film looked so fragile that we might have been looking at moving, barely moving, pictures of the court of Elizabeth I. Herbert Ponting's film of Scott's last expedition is older than this 1915 hand-cranked camera work, but survived better, I suppose, since it was kept in relative safety in the over-wintering hut at Cape Evans. Hurley's moving pictures only got as far as the moment when the

Endurance finally sank and they took off on an ice floe. Shackleton ordered the men to ditch as much as possible – he threw away the Bible apart from the fly-leaf signed by Queen Alexandra, Psalm 23 and the page from The Book of Job containing the lines:

> *Out of whose womb came the ice?*
> *And the hoary frost of Heaven, who hath gendered it?*
> *The waters are hid as with a stone.*
> *And the face of the deep is frozen.*

Hurley's cumbersome cinematograph didn't last long, so there is only still photography to record his time on Elephant Island. He kept the moving film of the early part of the journey as best he could, but even with modern restoration it looked as ancient as papyrus. The ship beset in the ice was covered with rime, grandiose and monumental, like a sculpture – it's a famous picture, but the movie version of the *Endurance* breaking up, creaking, wailing, sometimes seeming to scream as it buckled at the centre, with the main mast crashing to the deck and the whole thing finally sinking beneath the ice, is heart-stopping. When it was clear that the ship couldn't withstand the pressure, the dogs were dropped over the side on to a slide made out of a sail – a precursor to the emergency slide of planes. The dogs whined and barked, and slithered all out of control as the men below caught them, like fairground barkers, getting them on to the ice. There the dogs shook themselves in relief and ran rings around each other and the crew. Earlier, a scene showed the crew desperately trying to find a way through the closing ice. While some men hacked at the edges of the pack to make a split in the floe, others hauled on a rope to drag the ship through the narrow way that had been cut. The film was so frail at this point that the line of men and the rope between them seemed to bleed darkly into each other, blurring the individuals until they appeared to be umbilically attached to their own shadows. I glanced at John and saw he was near to weeping as we watched a final shot of Shackleton, on his last voyage, shampooing his pet Alsatian on the deck, sleeves rolled up, hugely enjoying himself. The next morning we would arrive at the place where, just days later, he was buried.

After the film, I had a coffee in the 'lounge' area, which was empty except for Janice. It was too late to avoid speaking to her. Janice had been a wraith throughout the trip. She was an Englishwoman in her thirties, travelling alone like me. I had spoken to her once or twice – she worked in an office and spent all her holidays and savings going to extraordinary and exotic places. And yet it was difficult to hold a conversation with Janice, who was about as chronically depressed, as far as I could see, as anyone I had ever met. Her face was set as if in perpetual mourning – the first time you saw her you thought she must have learned something catastrophic, a death in the family, and you wondered whether it would be fitting to go and try to console her. In fact, she looked like this always, and I and everyone else debated with ourselves about trying to be friendly with her. Several people had made an effort, but no

one more than once or twice before giving up. It was too difficult. She sat in silence and answered any questions or
comments made to her in a dull monotone. Still you were convinced that she must be convalescing from some personal
tragedy and yet there wasn't a hint of this, just the reiterated
story of her travels, with the rider that with this trip she had
been everywhere she ever wanted to go. She would have run
out of excitements as of the moment she set foot back on
shore at Ushuaia. Whenever I saw her on deck I tensed up for
fear that she was going to climb over the side. But she was not
histrionic in her behaviour, only in her implications. She
walked around the ship silently and alone, chain-smoking
because the woman who had been allocated to share her cabin
was a non-smoker.

'Hi,' I began, sitting down opposite Janice. 'Did you see the
film?'

'No,' she said, stubbed out her cigarette and walked away.

I think Janice is someone who lives deep, or perhaps not so
very deep, inside me. She seemed uncomfortably familiar and
frightening. Perhaps everyone felt this about her. When she
walked away, the relief was enormous.

It was bridge time. Staring time. Twice or three times a day I
wandered up to the top deck above my cabin and checked out
the instruments. Over the last couple of days, I'd figured out
how to read the monitor: the distance still to go to South
Georgia was 131 miles. We were doing 13.9 knots (whatever

that meant in m.p.h.) and our present position was 54° S, 41.59° W. Then I checked the pencilled line on the navigation chart to see where we were in the world. This had become a necessary ritual, but after that I went through to the navigation deck and did what I really liked doing, which was to stand by the panoramic glass windscreen and stare out to sea. The captain was rarely on the bridge, only when there was manoeuvring to be done; the plain cruising was left to the two men on watch. One of them stood at the wheel – though it was actually a small semicircle, not the satisfactory great wagon wheel of my assumptions – leaning the small of his back against a padded post a bit like a shooting stick. The other Russian stood at the windscreen most of the time, occasionally looking into the radar sight, or at other incomprehensible instruments. Nothing he saw ever seemed to excite him. The watches were two-hour stints and so far every pair I had come across remained silent, except for an odd murmured comment in Russian about what seemed nothing in particular, and a grunted response. Clearly the point of being on watch was to watch out, and this was what they did, but it takes a particular kind of person to be content to stand and stare out at an uneventful sea for two hours at a time. It takes a person like me, for example. I began to think that to be one of these sailors would suit me down to the ground. I stood out of their way on the left side of the windscreen and gazed at sky, waves and the occasional albatross wheeling around the bow, and they stood, the wheel man dead centre, the other on the far right, doing exactly the same.

They both had that unfocused, dream look in their eyes, as doubtless had I, and neither felt the need to do anything at all except the bare minimum to keep the ship on course. Presumably that was mostly done by computer anyway, so they were only there for emergencies. Though they were dreamy, they remained watchful. It was quite an easy state to get into. I silently wondered, if the earth was flat and of infinite extent would you see a horizon? Though I didn't wonder so hard that I required an answer. The sailors on watch ignored me, apart from an initial nod as I arrived, and my nod as I left. The bridge felt as much like home as my cabin; the place where I could do what I most wanted to do without anyone either stopping me or noticing what I was doing. It was as close to being alone in the ocean as it was possible to get in a space containing three people. Staring at the horizon – the earth is not flat nor of infinite extent – I tried hard to imagine the death certificate that Chloe had found as being that of my mother. What did I feel? Nothing . . . and then a shock: if she is dead, then she has been alive all those intervening years, living, breathing, sharing the same air on the same planet. Her death would indicate her previous life, and this was quite a disturbing thought. Not as disturbing, perhaps, as Chloe *not* finding a death certificate, but still, it would change the world I thought I had lived in, if nothing else. A little abstract this, but approaching the concrete rather too closely for my liking. The unanswerable (to me) question about the horizon seemed a more attractive line of thought, and I went back to it and the line cutting between sea and sky, with a return of some tranquillity. The bridge was almost uncannily silent. Oh, I do want to be a sailor.

At nine the next morning we geared up – thermal underwear, cashmere sweater (useful already), wellies, waterproofs, gloves and a lifejacket complete with whistle – and clambered down the bobbing gangway on to the thrumming Zodiac. The sky was brilliant blue, the sea as flat as a pancake and blue as the sky. I sweltered as we zoomed along at sea level, a rubber boat on a pond, towards the jetty. Marjorie, an amused retired economist from Oregon whose husband had been taken ill suddenly and so was unable to join her, sat next to me. She was very small, and bundled up in her wet weather gear looked like a canary yellow version of the murderous dwarf in *Don't Look Now*. Not that I'm exactly willowy, and doubtless I myself resembled a sea-green Munchkin. As the man in the Survival Shop in London said to me severely, as I pulled a face at the sight of myself waterproofed up in the mirror: 'You're not supposed to be making a fashion statement, you know.' Still, it's a good thing there were no mirrors in the mud room where we put on our togs.

Marjorie and I congratulated each other on the balmy conditions. Our leader Butch had spent some time warning us to put on plenty of clothes and take very great care to follow instructions for getting on to the Zodiacs. 'We have never suffered from a fatality up to this point in time,' he said with knitted brow, but that was because all previous expeditioners (that was us, we were no tourists) had followed orders 'to the letter and the spirit'. Marjorie and I shared a distaste for being ordered to follow orders, and whispered mutinously that it was easy-peasy, why the fuss?

As far as I can see South Georgia is further away from anywhere than anywhere else in the world. It's 1,100 miles from South America. The Antarctic Peninsula is just two days away from Ushuaia, while it had taken three days and nights to get to Grytviken. Although, as the British government sees it, South Georgia is part of the Falklands Dependencies, it's actually 1,290 miles from the Falkland Islands. As a whaling station it thrived, but it's a mystery why anyone would go to war over it once whaling was over, until you remember the oil in the surrounding waters (as well as around the Peninsula), and that the hands-off clause in the Antarctic Treaty runs out in twenty years' time. South Georgia's convenience for processing and distributing the liquid billions is obvious. You didn't really think that little skirmish with the Argentinians was about honour, did you?

The abandoned whaling station at Grytviken is either lovingly preserved in its natural state or derelict, depending on how you choose to look at it. If derelict landscapes, like the murkier parts of King's Cross and the old unreconstructed docklands appeal, then Grytviken is a pearl of desolation. A rust-bucket ghost town, left to rot in its own beautiful way. Approached from the bay in the Zodiac, it was a small hamlet of white-walled, red-roofed one- and two-storey buildings nestling on the handkerchief-sized edge of the island, surrounded on all sides by rising black volcanic mountains, topped with white and smeared with snow and ice in the dips and crevasses. It looked idyllic, if a little vulnerable, as if a brave attempt at human assertion were being pushed ineluctably into the sea by the encroaching island itself. Once we were close up we could see that a different aspect of nature had taken command, as the neat white houses turned out mostly to be decaying sheds and warehouses, stained by weather, with rotting doors hanging off rusting hinges, dotted inside with broken and corroded implements and hefty languishing chains. It was a lovely place, as I stepped on to the decaying planking of the flensing plan, where the whales were hefted up and tiny men with hockey stick-shaped knives at the end of a long pole took their positions around the bulk of the dead mammal and carved away the inches-thick layer of blubber from the flesh. It was a town memorializing the efficiency of commerce. We wandered around and discovered this place for the rendering of the blubber, that for the butchering of the flesh, another for the processing of the bones. A purposeful place made beautiful by its dereliction and the delicate carvings and ornately cut patterns of rust on iron. A couple of dead hulks of half-sunk whaling ships to either side of the inlet finished off the symmetry of decline.

We were greeted by a ruddy-faced Englishman in a fisherman's sweater and his hearty wife, though my attention was gripped by the surreal sight of three soldiers in camouflage fatigues yomping past, holding fierce-looking automatic weapons at the ready. It looked like newsfilm of troop manoeuvres in Northern Ireland. The soldiers flashed past as it was my turn to receive a rugged handshake from the ruddy-faced man. He was the curator of the museum, the only spick and span building in town. We were warned to be careful where we walked, because floors and ceilings were likely to cave in, and not to walk towards the cluster of buildings a mile to the right, on King Edward Point, which was the British Garrison and a military secret. How many soldiers were stationed there? This was a military secret, too. 'Very hush hush,' said the ruddy-faced curator solemnly. We could, however, walk as far to the left as we wished (though without losing sight of at least one of the expedition team), and were very welcome to tour the museum and visit the island shop.

The day was balmy, and as we were here for three hours or so, we stripped off our lifejackets and waterproofs and stowed them in an old wash-house. After enjoying the bleakness and beauty of the buildings, I walked along the shore towards the hill half a mile to the left, which sported a low white picket fence, of the sort that surrounds an English country garden. On the way, I encountered my first elephant seals which lay dotted in small crowds and sometimes alone along the shore. You didn't notice them at first, because they look like part of the landscape. But once you've identified their grey hulks as living creatures, often by getting a mite too close and getting an open-mouthed, ill-tempered belch from one of them, you came to a finer understanding of the force of gravity.

Trapped between evolution's two primary rules of fitness and sexual selection, the bull elephant seal slumps sulkily by the edges of the sea. Evolution must have scratched its head, a little embarrassed at this particularly inelegant solution to its own logic, but come to the conclusion that rules are rules. People from the boat called them ugly, but that doesn't quite catch the aesthetic disaster of the elephant seal. It is more that they are utterly ill-suited for this planet. They might, it occurred to me, have been dropped or fallen from an alien vessel and landed – splat – as we saw them, on the sea shore, to do the best they could in difficult circumstances. Gravity bore down on their enormous bulk (a big bull seal can be up to twenty-two feet long), in the same way that large stones are piled up to squash pressed beef. A grey jellied mountain results, whose sides slope down to their inadequate-looking flippers. One more stone on the pile of gravity and the whole strained substance would rupture, exploding flesh and blubber through its skin for miles around. They lay around as if exhausted, which I suppose they were, their relatively small heads sunk wearily on the black sand. The females and babies had the anthropomorphic advantage of huge, round wet eyes which rolled wide open as someone passed them by, with a fatigued but appealing look as if to say 'Can you imagine?' The cows and pups turned on to their stomachs to scratch their bellies idly with the claws at the end of their flippers, so you began to think, 'Well, maybe it's not so bad.' The bulls didn't roll; the attempt to move their mountain of flesh would probably have burst their hearts. And while they might have just as corny eyes, I hardly noticed them because of my disbelief at the sight of the truncated trunks from which they get

142

their name. Elephant seal is one of those euphemistic names humans give creatures who remind them of what they don't want to be reminded of. If an honest name were to be given, they would be flaccid penis seal, because the wrinkled concertinaed length and the bobbing, swinging floppiness of those extended noses is a satire on the male reproductive member. You would, if you were that way inclined, shield your children's eyes from the sight.

Doubtless the creatures were a marvel of grace under the water, their shape ergonomic for cutting through the currents, their layers of blubber keeping them warm in the freezing sea, but on land they were strapped and stranded. They had to be on land to mate and breed – a bit of a Heath Robinson solution on the part of evolution since whales manage to do it all in the water – but the size of the bulls, which makes them so exquisitely desirable to the cows, disables them. They moved by lurching their bulk forward, arching their heads and giving a pitiful heave towards where they were not with their inadequate flippers. Not unreasonably, they huffed and puffed with every motion, but they did get along in their fashion when they really needed to. They only need to when they want to get back into the sea, on top of a cow or to defend their harem against some other encroaching leviathan. Given their bulk, the bulls only move when absolutely necessary. We were warned not to get closer than six feet to any of the animals we might come across, but the bulls were so still on the sand, it was sometimes impossible to spot them, and once or twice I found myself within a foot or two of a boulder that suddenly

143

opened its eyes, raised its head, making the trunk swing
obscenely and then yawned a silent threat at me to keep my
distance. Nothing is so red, moist and fleshy as the inside of
the mouth of an elephant seal. With the trunk flapping above
the scarlet cavern of its mouth, the story of sexual reproduc-
tion is laid bare. You are not so much terrified at the sight as
petrified by the absurd obscenity. When the bulls do make a
deliberate noise, while they're mating or fighting, they produce
from the depths of their blubbery quivering throats a cracking
belch so sonorous and amplified that it echoes off the sides of
the mountains, and thus completes the sense that you are
observing a living visual and aural exemplar of the seven
deadly sins. This is God the popular songwriter:

> Would you like to swing on a star
> Carry moonbeams home in a jar
> And be better off than you are?
> Or would you rather be an Elephant Seal?

Me, I'd rather carry moonbeams home in a jar.

Elephant seals being what they are, and modern travellers
being what they are, the photography had begun in earnest.
The debate about taking a camera with me on this trip raged
for weeks. I've never owned a camera, never taken one on holiday. Roger-the-Ex, however, is a fervent and fine
photographer. He and Chloe, and just about everyone else,
insisted that I take a camera with me. How could I go so far, to
such an out-of-the-way place with such out-of-the-way sights

without taking photos? Easy, I say. I like looking at stuff. You have to stop looking in order to point a camera at something. And why peer through a lens which limits your vision? You can't see if you're always composing what's in front of you into a fancy shot. Anyway, I hate having a camera hanging about my neck. Just something else to fuss about. I reminded Chloe of the hours we spent trying to be enthusiastic about Roger's rolls and rolls of admittedly stunning holiday snaps. Even so, it would be perverse not to take one.

Roger brought round what he called a really simple camera. It weighed as much as a single-decker bus, had two bulky lenses which had to be screwed on and off the camera body according to the subject, and had enough scales of numbers for this and that to calculate the trajectory of the stars. I intended to be good and take it, but when I tried to practise the elementary changing of the lenses, I failed. It's just a knack, Roger explained. I didn't have it. When no one was looking, I hid the camera in its small padded suitcase behind the Hoover under the stairs and took off without it. My courage failed at the airport. I bought the smallest most automatic camera that the duty-free shop could sell me. It zoomed itself, adjusted itself for light and focus and wound itself on. It also fitted into my pocket. A compromise. So far I hadn't used it, and I had forgotten to take it with me on the Zodiac.

Everyone else, however, was snapping off film like there was no tomorrow, let alone two more weeks of touring. One woman had brought eighty rolls of film with her from the States. People were weighed down on each shoulder with spare lenses, light meters, and those lucky enough to have wives or husbands handy let them carry tripods one pace behind like native bearers. The most offensive person on the trip was a Scandinavian professional photographer, getting shots for a new book. He elbowed people out of his way, commandeered swathes of space, stuck his camera into the creatures' faces for the big close-ups, and ran busily everywhere in search of the telling shot. He was as single focused as a camera lens, but some of the unprofessional others came close. It wasn't just still photography, of course. The camcorder was much in evidence, so, added to the click and whirr of motorized snapping, was the monotonous murmuring of voices, not people in conversation with each other, but individuals talking into their machines, adding commentary to their motion pictures. Every time I heard what I thought was someone talking behind me and politely turned round to listen, I saw a Cyclops with video camera replacing the missing eye, pacing deliberately about, moving the machine and their head up and down and around, as if eyes no longer swivelled in their sockets, muttering into their chests. To anyone not aware of the purpose of the camcorder, we would have been mistaken for an outing of the deranged. Of course, people were not actually talking to themselves, nor even thinking aloud, but talking to their friends and family at some time in the future when they would be sitting in their living rooms watching the video. The present experience was already in the past for them, they had skipped over time, and were seeing the world through their video lenses, as it would look when the current moment was dead and gone.

Things were named and described, sentences formed, a final draft written, without that first-draft struggle to transform wordless impressions into language. There was no translation of world into words, just the direct commentary, cutting out all the processes that might have added up to reflection. The memories being created now would exist, frozen in the future as lens-framed news reports.

Memory, as far as I can make out, does not have a particular location in the brain, as was once thought, but resides in discrete packets dotted all over the place. Or it doesn't reside anywhere, except in the remembering itself, when the memory is created from the bits of experience stored around the brain. Memory is continually created, a story told and retold, using jigsaw pieces of experience. It's utterly unreliable in some ways, because who can say whether the feeling or emotion that seems to belong to the recollection actually belongs to it rather than being available from the general store of likely emotions we have learned? Who can say that this image is correct, and not an image from a book or film or a picture, another part of one's life, which, seeming to fit with the general story, is pressed into service? Memory is not false in the sense that it is wilfully bad, but it is excitingly corrupt in its inclination to make a proper story of the past. Photos fix the past, or snippets of it. Film or video fix the past even more firmly, giving us movement and voices, leaving less and less to the imagination. The difference between radio and television, perhaps. But even then something is always missing of the reality of the experienced moment, I think. It is odd to look at

147

photos you have taken of a place you have been to. Something essential has gone, making the photo make the experience seem more rather than less remote.

I have a single photograph of my mother. It was taken after we had left Paramount Court, before the social workers and the University College Hospital shrinks sent me to boarding school, when she and I were living in the room in Mornington Crescent. She and I are in Trafalgar Square. I would have been eleven. The photograph was taken by one of those professional photographers who snap tourists. My mother and I are standing shoulder to shoulder, our arms around each other's backs. Already I am as tall as her; she was barely five foot. I am, in the photo, what I was supposed to be. My hair is in plaits falling on to the front of my shoulders. The end of each plait is tied with wide ribbon into a bow. I have on a pale shirtwaister dress which falls below my knees, and a cardigan over it. I'm wearing thonged sandals so it must have been a sunny day, but for all that, my hands are covered in short white gloves. Very smart, very nice, my mother would have thought. She is in a floral frock, belted at the waist and falling almost to her ankles as all her dresses did to hide the scar on one of her legs from a road accident that happened before I was born. Her hair is dark and permed short, and she is wearing wrist-length white gloves like me. Around us pigeons are walking about, and the Square is dotted with people in summer frocks and shirt sleeves. The black and white photo is faded, of course, and our faces are in shadow from the late afternoon sun behind us. My face is long and angular, hers is more rounded – now I think about it, she called it heart-shaped – but there is something sharp about her features. She is smiling directly into the camera, a posterity smile, a mother who is content to be with her daughter. My head is tipped slightly down, my chin towards my chest, and I am looking up, I now realize, with that Princess of Wales upward glance – shy or sly, hard to decide. I think there is the ghost of a smile on my face, but it's more shadowed than my mother's and it is a little difficult to tell. At our feet, extending along the ground and uninterrupted by pigeons, our shadows form a single elongated blot on the otherwise sunny macadam. It is a coalesced shadow, we are standing too close for the sun to slip between our bodies. Her shadow and mine blur together into a unified shape, as umbilical as the creaky film of Shackleton's roped-together men trying to pull the *Endurance* through the ice floe.

Just before this picture was taken, I had been in a local authority home for a month or six weeks, somewhere by the sea. I don't remember where, but I recall walking in crocodile formation along cliffs with the sea to my right. My mother was signed up for social security by the social worker and found the bedsitting room. They also persuaded her that it would be a good idea if I went to the boarding school. A progressive, co-ed, vegetarian Quaker private school which took a few problem children paid for by their local authorities who were deemed too bright to go to the authority's schools for mal-adjusted children. It didn't work out so well. My mother kept turning up at the school in Hertfordshire and screaming either at me or at the staff about them keeping me from her and about me deserting her. After a term and a half, they asked me to leave because they couldn't deal with the disruption my mother caused. Later, aged thirteen, after I had found my vanished father and went to live with him, I went back to the school, having discovered to my bitter disappointment, that my father was not the man I remembered. That didn't work out so well either. I was expelled, this time on my own account, for general waywardness, after eighteen months. Thereafter, in quick succession, to Banbury, unsuccessfully, to my father; then off to my mother equally unsuccessfully; then into the hospital in Hove.

None of this is evident or foreshadowed in the photo of my mother and I in Trafalgar Square on a sunny day, except perhaps in the darkness over our faces, but that, of course, is nothing more than a retrospective conceit.

I wondered, too, whether it was possible to experience anything fresh any more. If there was a moment of marvelling, it was in the amazing closeness of the reality to what I had already seen in other media. Sometimes, looking out to sea, I had to shake away the films I had seen, the sense of remembering, without having ever actually experienced the event. I had seen such a sea many times on television, film and in photographs. The sea outside my cabin window looked remarkably like those pictures. It was, well, a copy. And here we all were, taking films of what we had already seen on film so that our children and grandchildren and our friends would once again not see it all afresh for themselves. And if they do go off to strange places, it will be, like us, to confirm what is already known. To see again, in nature, what has been seen already in hi-fidelity, sound-surround, full-coloured vista-vision.

Still, wasn't I delighted to see Hurley's film of the *Endurance* expedition? Didn't I have a sense that I was peeping through a keyhole directly into the past? A privilege was how I thought of it just the previous night. This was what the snappers were doing. Capturing memories, not just for themselves, but probably imagining their grandchildren and their children watching the present moment that their ancestors had brought back for them. Ponting made Scott, Wilson, Oates and Bowers play-act a night on the final polar attempt. They set up a tent, cooked hoosh, smoked, joked and then snuggled down into their reindeer sleeping bags for the night, all in broad daylight, at Cape Evans, well before setting off on the actual attempt from which no one returned. It makes strange viewing. Those men you know are going to die, acting it out as it ought to have been, rather than how it would be – a little hammily, full of embarrassed good humour. But the real drama of their deaths went unrecorded except by their own self-conscious words, carefully drafted to ensure the future remembered them in the right way. Which it did for a while. A camera would have recorded Scott's tantrums and bad-temper with Oates for not making the final sacrifice in good time. It would have shown the arguments the men had about whether or not to take Dr Wilson's morphine tablets, and if indeed they were actually taken. It might have shown up fallible, frightened men at the ends of their tether. Thus a generation would have lost a myth, while another generation would have been deprived of the satisfaction of debunking it.

But the photography does more than push the present out of the way and possibly make memory even more unreliably your own than ever. It also captures a slice of the world, makes it private territory, deprives others of the right of access. Photography is a modern, miniature form of colonization. There were about seventy people wandering about this deserted spot, plenty of room and lots of places to go. It didn't represent a crowd. But all the time, I and others had to duck and swerve to avoid the triangle of the world the pointed lenses were capturing. The world was being snapped up all around me. 'Sorry', 'Excuse me' we apologized to each other as we stepped across the invisible boundary belonging to each photographer. Sometimes I was invited inside the private wedge of world to participate in the picture or film, but then I had to behave, or pose rather than simply walk through the space. If there were enough photographers standing in the right positions, there was almost nowhere to walk without feeling I was encroaching. Odd that. And I was genuinely apologetic about getting in their way. I didn't want to spoil anyone's picture. Yet, this piece of wilderness belonged to no one, and one of the pleasures of wilderness is thoughtlessly wandering through it. Now Grytviken was as parcelled up as if it were divided by seventy picket fences like the one I was making for on the lower ridge of the mountain.

'Hey, Jenny, can you stand by that bull seal so I can show the scale of the thing?' called Big Jim, whose camera was suited to his size. I obliged so that folks back home near Palm Springs would see how enormous the seals are in the Sub-Antarctic. I suppose they will also see what middle-aged Londoners look like on a sunny day in South Georgia.

'Who's that, Jim?'

'She was one of the trippers. A Brit. A real Cockney accent. Writing a book she said.'

Oh yes, so I am. And here is my way of colonizing the world. Hi, Jim.

I met Phoenix John coming down as I climbed the hill to the white picket fence. He shook his head at me, wordless at the achievement of a dream. The small fence surrounded Grytviken's graveyard where past whalers were buried under neat white low headstones. Two had died of diphtheria in 1910; a dozen or more from a typhus outbreak in 1912. Others would have died from accidents or the effects of drink. The pastor of the church built there in 1913 acknowledged 'religious life among the whalers left much to be desired'. I, like John, had climbed the hill to see Shackleton's grave and it was immediately obvious, the tall hewn granite post, with '*Ernest Henry Shackleton, Explorer*', carved on it, and fresh alpine flowers at its foot. But another grave caught my eye, at right angles to Shackleton. It had a low white headstone, but unlike the rest a rough wooden cross stood over it. It too had fresh pink flowers and was the only other grave apart from

Shackleton's to have been regularly and carefully tended. The
words burned into the wooden cross read

RIP

FELIX 26.04.82 ARTUSO

Beneath the horizontal of the cross under the name was a
small painted rectangle made of a single white stripe sand-
wiched between two pale blue ones. Unhappy Felix had died
not so long ago, and the rectangle was, it dawned on me, the
Argentinian flag. I had forgotten about South Georgia's par-
ticipation in the Falklands War. I remembered that two
women naturalists were stranded for the duration of the war in
one of its deserted bays, filming penguins, remaining in
hiding, but I didn't recollect much else of what happened very
clearly. I tried to recall it on the way down the hill, wondering
about Felix and his immaculate grave. At the museum building two soldiers sat on the steps leading up to the doorway. I
said 'hello' as I passed.

'You're English,' one of them declared as a shipwrecked
British traveller might greet his rescuer with extra pleasure.
'We don't get many of us arriving at South Georgia. It's a real
pleasure to hear your accent.'

He was in his mid-twenties and his name was Andy (his
friend's name was Scot, which I was to remember is spelt with
one 't'). He was very eager to talk. Both men had rifles resting
at their feet. SA80s, they told me. They were Royal Engineers
doing a five-month tour of South Georgia. This was Andy's

second tour. Before that he had been in Northern Ireland. This was a pretty boring posting, he explained. He and his girlfriend had just split up, but he didn't really blame her. Eleven months is a long time to be separate and faithful, he conceded. Andy was from Southend; Scot, a younger man of few words, came from Hemel Hempstead.

'Why are you patrolling around with guns?' I asked.

'Making sure they can be seen,' Andy told me.

'By whom?'

'The Argys. There's been a rumour going around that the troops here don't have any arms, so we've been making them visible.'

I looked around at the bay, which was deserted apart from the two half-sunken whalers and the white ship awaiting our return.

'Who's looking?'

'Spies on the ships. We've got to let them know not to mess with us.'

'I thought the Argentinians were buying up the Falklands.'

'I bet they'd rather get it for nothing. They've made a £1 million offer to each farmholder on the Falklands. They say about half of them are prepared to accept. But our government wouldn't allow it even if all the islanders agreed. It's a matter of principle.'

I didn't know about that. I could see how the Falkland Islanders might be tempted by a million quid for their draughty out-of-the-way sheep farms. Pity it couldn't have happened in 1982 and prevented a lot of unnecessary deaths and the tainted glory of Margaret Thatcher. Still, Andy and I were not likely to agree about politics, and he was so eager for British company that I kept quiet. He'd had enough of the boredom of this life and had applied to do a course in bomb disposal. When he'd finished, he'd be posted to Bosnia. What he'd really wanted was to join the Southend Fire Brigade, but there was a two-year waiting list. After nine years in the Army, he was anxious to do something different.

I asked him about Felix Artuso, up on the hill. He reminded me how South Georgia was taken by a small group of Argentinian soldiers posing as scrap-metal merchants. Fourteen marines went into hiding and then fought them off. Fifteen Argentinians were killed, according to Andy, though the official number was three. Young Felix Artuso was one of them. A marine came face to face with him and thinking he was going for a gun, shot first. It turned out that Felix was unarmed.

'It's what happens in war,' said Andy sorrowfully, speaking very respectfully of Artuso, like a fallen comrade. 'His parents wanted him to be buried on South Georgia. The Brits buried him with full military honours. It's the way we do things.'

Since the war, three soldiers had died on South Georgia. One saved his two cans allowance of beer a night for a Friday piss-up and thought he could swim across the bay. He froze to death in about seven minutes. Another also got drunk and fell during an inadvisable walk in the middle of the night, dying of exposure. An Irish Ranger died from cold and injuries while trying to climb one of the mountains on his own.

'The boredom gets to you,' explains Andy. 'It was really nice to talk to someone from home.'

His walkie-talkie crackled, and military orders were conveyed. Doubtless it was time for another yomp in case the spies were watching. I wandered into the museum which was full of blackened iron cauldrons and whale-butchering implements. My fellow travellers tut-tutted away and averted their eyes from the postcards of whales being stripped. T-shirts, tea-towels, ashtrays and maps were also available in the shop to prove how far I had been. I bought several T-shirts with garish king penguins on the front for Chloe and her friends who were looking after the flat. They wouldn't wear them but they'd be pleased to have something from so far away. Better than tea-towels. For myself I got three copies of a postcard of Shackleton, his hair parted in the middle and slicked down, looking uncomfortable in front of the camera, but wonderfully handsome in a rugged way. He looked as roguish as he seems to have been. A bit of a con man, who took off on the *Endurance* expedition before the money was actually available, leaving others to sort out the mess. Something of a ladies' man he was, in his charming Irish way. Brother Frank went the whole way and was actually imprisoned for some financial shenanigans with the English aristocracy. I'd developed a real soft spot for Shackleton.

I almost found myself in an argument with a severe Englishwoman about whether it was right for Scott to forbid Shackleton to use McMurdo Sound as his base during his bid for the pole. Scott had found it during his first expedition, and he hated Shackleton – not a gentleman, and too popular with the lower ranks. Shackleton was mortified, his word having been given, when he had to anchor at McMurdo because of the lethal weather conditions. What right had Scott to veto a bay on the Antarctic mainland to another explorer? Every right, said my English companion sternly. 'He found it. It was his.' A veritable Scott/Shackleton feud threatened to break out as I insisted that it was disgraceful of Scott to behave so miserably. 'A man's word is his word,' said my opponent, inviting some riposte about a word given under duress being unkeepable in life-threatening circumstances, but I knew I was out of my depth in these very strong feelings about long dead men. I did not wish to feel very strongly about them.

It was beginning to rain, and the sky was darkening. The glorious sunshine instantly became a thing of the past. I began to see that things might be surprisingly changeable around those parts. As the wind got up, Grytviken was suddenly a dour, deserted place. For the first time I started to feel cold and damp. It happened from one moment to the next. A small shiver of bleakness that was not entirely related to the weather ran through me. I felt quite happy to get into one of the first returning Zodiacs and head back for Cabin 532. My first landing had been neither white nor solitary.

By the afternoon, the world had turned industrial grey. While we were having lunch, the ship sailed a short distance south, lurching through a disturbed sea, down to St Andrew's Bay for our second scheduled landing. As we queued up along the deck by the gangway the wind and rain soaked us, testing our water- and wind-proof gear for the first time. Below the gangway, the Zodiacs bounced like bucking ponies in the decidedly choppy waves. This was an altogether different experience from the morning landing. The colour of the sky and sea had darkened to a uniform shade of iron. It was as if the sun had never shone, nor ever would again. The wind and waves did an angry *pas de deux*, and the rain stabbed sideways. Butch stood heroically on the undulating gangway landing looking solemn, shouting through cupped hands across the wind to the driver of the first Zodiac. There was some doubt about whether we were going to get ashore. It seemed that the windspeed was close to the maximum allowed for landings. It certainly whipped up the sea quite fiercely against the side of the ship, flinging it over the black rubber sides of the Zodiacs. The rain nicked us sharply in the face as we waited for a decision to be made.

We were to go. St Andrew's Bay was the great penguin treat of the trip. We were warned that the landing would be cut short if the wind got any worse. The gangway was wet, slippery and lurched up and down. The sailor's handshake at the bottom was gratefully received, proving its worth as I stepped gingerly across blowy nothingness into the shiny wet Zodiac. We weren't watching the sea now, we were on it, down at its level, rising and falling with every wave. While I waited for the others to get on the boat, the layers of waterproofing kept me dry and not particularly cold, except for my face, which was soaking and icy from the rain and tingling from the wind. It was beginning to feel like an adventure as Marjorie arrived, looking a bit alarmed, to sit on the edge of the Zodiac next to me, and we grasped the rope that ran along just behind us. It took about fifteen minutes to get to the shore as the dinghy tacked and swerved to avoid the worst of the head-on wind. Even so the raised front of the boat caught an angry wave every few minutes and saturated us. The edge we sat on was quite wide, but didn't feel wide enough as we rolled and some-times leaped about in the now stormy sea. We had to keep our heads lowered or the rain and spray blinded us. It was, how-ever, the most exhilarating ride I've ever had, fast and furious, the motor buzzing angrily against a wind that howled past my ears and made my eyes water salt tears to match the salt spray drenching my face. We were so close to it, intimate now with the movement of the waves, the weather, the Antarctic sea. When not lying on my bunk or staring out from the bridge, I'd choose this. From time to time when we smacked into a big wave, I laughed out loud.

As we approached the slightly protected bay, the wind let up a little and it was possible to look up, straight ahead towards the land. We were being watched. The long shoreline and the beach right back to the glacier and mountains were packed so tight with penguins that they formed a continuous carpet. A legion of black faces and orange beaks pointed out to sea facing in our direction, seeming to observe our arrival. St Andrew's Bay is famously the breeding ground for 100,000 king penguins (I don't know who counted but I'm not inclined to argue), and there they all were, standing in serried ranks, watching without curiosity as half a dozen black rubber dinghies came towards them. To us, they did seem to be watching, but then again, quantum physics notwithstanding, if we hadn't been approaching the shore, if the sea had been deserted, they would still all be standing there looking out to sea. That's what penguins do. Stand. Every year, for thousands of years, for hundreds of thousands of years for all I know, 100,000 penguins stand along this beach, mating and incubating eggs. One day, once a year or so, black rubber dinghies approach, and a handful of people come to the bay, believing that the penguins are watching them arrive. For the penguins, it's just another day of standing and staring. They were not even slightly interested at our approach. We made a wet landing in knee-deep icy water and clambered up on to the rocky land. The penguins parted slightly to make way for us, but they still stood looking out to sea. The fact is, that on land the only thing a penguin has to fear are the swooping skuas, diving through the air for their eggs and chicks. Danger comes from above, not from the sea or the land. It seemed that they didn't even compute humans and their noisy boats. We were not part of their existence, presented no obvious danger and therefore were ignored, quite overlooked. You could walk right up to them and they would take no notice. If you stood in their way as they waddled along their track from nest to sea to feed, they stopped a few inches from your feet and made a small, semicircular detour around you, as they would if they found a boulder in their way. If you got down on your knees and faced them eyeball to eyeball, they looked back, turning an eye towards you, but deciding what you were not, lost interest rapidly.

I was very taken with this timeless standing, unwitnessed, unwitnessing, that we were interrupting, though only barely. That was the point, for me, of Antarctica: that it was simply there, always had been, always would be, with great tracts of the continent unseen, unwitnessed, cycling through its two seasons, the ice rolling slowly from the centre to the edges where eventually it breaks off. A place that is and always has been unseen. Now these penguins, getting on with what they do, standing in their place. And on this or that day, a group of people arrive for a visit and make not the slightest difference to anything at all. South Georgia is so out of the way that fewer people visit it than the Antarctic mainland. Only a couple of hundred people a year arrived at Grytviken, fewer still, I imagine, land at St Andrew's Bay. I ached for the endurance and the indifference of this landscape and its penguin inhabitants.

My fellow travellers were filming and photographing up a storm. The word 'cute' was heard for the first time, but multiplied like an echo. Penguins, in fact, are cute. They have a ridiculous dignity to our eyes: upstanding, busy creatures, who are hopelessly designed for life on land, but seem determined to overcome their disability. They waddle furiously about their business, marching in orderly lines along set tracks down to the sea to get food for themselves and their mates. But every now and again they drop the front, as we might if we thought we were alone and unobserved, and, finding it tedious walking down an incline, take to their bellies and slide down

162

the slippery slope. Poised between fake dignity and letting their hair down, they seem remarkably like caricatures of ourselves. So they make us laugh, as children do. Penguins, you can be sure, don't see things this way, but quantum physics withstanding this time, it's us doing the looking. It's impossible not to be anthropomorphic, and I'm not sure why we should try. I don't really believe that the penguins are damaged by our self-centred view of them, providing they are left alone to get on with their lives. Relating the natural world to ourselves is what we do, just as standing staring out to sea is what penguins do.

However, it was fairly clear that penguin life is not that cute. The skuas wheeled overhead waiting for an opportunity to take what they could. And the standing and staring became on close inspection a frantic business. The colony was full of fevered activity. Lines of penguins marched back and forth to the shore, up and down impossibly steep inclines, in order to provide for their mates and their offspring. Once in the sea they are vulnerable to seals. On land, if a mate doesn't return from foraging, the brooding penguin and its hard-worked-for egg will die of starvation. In the middle of the beach, as I began to walk along it, there was an empty space in the centre of which a penguin stood perfectly still, while eighteen inches away a large grey and white skua sat with monumental patience. They ignored each other, at least in the sense that neither looked at or took notice of the other. It seemed charming, two creatures at ease with each other, veritable lion laying down with the lamb stuff, until I got closer and saw a great

163

florid gash running down the penguin's side. The skua was waiting for the penguin's final, inevitable collapse, to provide it and its young with an easy and very substantial meal. To be entirely anthropomorphic about it, the sight was heartbreaking. It's not much of a life being a penguin.

The weather had worsened. It was now dark, as if dusk had fallen, a twilight that in this Antarctic summer does not occur. The clouds appeared to be just a few feet above our heads, and were black and heavy, fast moving as the wind hurried them along. The sand was black, volcanic residue, the cliffs soared darkly, the glacier was a dull grey, and the sea slate. A planet turned ominous. The wind picked up alarmingly, so that I was not walking along the beach, but pushing through resistant air. As the wind increased I could actually lean into it, lean on it at what seemed an impossible angle without falling. It came in long gusts, suddenly dropping and leaving me stumbling in mid-air, having to regain my balance. It was not just substantial, but sharp, even wilful. It picked up the black sand and hurled it painfully against my face. And now it was getting really cold. It was an odd sort of cold, because it wasn't exactly the air that was cold, or coldest, but like the sand, the wind carried icy blasts from the glacier and threw them against you like pointed sticks. This hurt more than the sand hitting my face. It was also now no longer raining but sleeting horizontally. My eyes wept, my nose ran, and within a few minutes I had a sharp pain in my left eye which radiated down my cheek, although it wasn't pain, it was cold such as I hadn't ever experienced. Cold as pain rather than mere discomfort. Until now only my unprotected face had suffered. The layers of silk thermal underwear and two pairs of socks, wool T-shirt, cashmere sweater, windproof jacket and foam lifevest had been doing their stuff. But gradually the protection was breeched. After fifteen or twenty minutes walking along the beach, the wet and icy blasts began to seep through the layers as if they were merely gauze. When it reached the flesh, I felt I had an inkling of what it means to be cold, but then it went deeper, and after half an hour it had gone beyond the skin and directly into the bones. My very marrow was chilled, I felt iced and saturated from head to foot. It was as if the wind, having got my measure, was denying my existence and simply rattling through me. I have never felt so unprotected in my life as in that bleak, dark landscape where there is absolutely nowhere to shelter. Only in those dreams where you find yourself walking naked down a busy street have I felt as vulnerable.

But this was not really cold, not serious. Apsley Cherry-Garrard on his winter journey to collect emperor penguin eggs, speaks of a temperature of 70 below, which is meaningless if you are sitting reading about it in an armchair, until he describes a night of shivering in his sleeping bag:

> For me it was a very bad night: a succession of shivering fits which I was quite unable to stop, and which took possession of my body for many minutes at a time until I thought my back would break, such was the strain placed upon it. They talk of chattering teeth: but when

165

your body chatters you may call yourself cold. I can only compare the strain to that which I have been unfortunate enough to see in a case of lock-jaw.

Cherry-Garrard is not one for exaggeration.

I have met with amusement people who say, 'Oh, we had minus fifty temperatures in Canada; they didn't worry me,' or 'I've been down to minus sixty something in Siberia.' And then you find that they had nice dry clothing, a nice night's sleep in a nice aired bed, and had just walked out after lunch for a few minutes from a nice warm hut or an overheated train. And they look back upon it as an experience to be remembered. Well! Of course as an experience of cold this can only be compared to eating a vanilla ice with hot chocolate cream after an excellent dinner at Claridge's. But in our present state we began to look upon minus fifties as a luxury which we did not often get.

So it wasn't really cold, wet and bleak on the beach at St Andrew's Bay. But for a couple of hours *I* was all those things. I am very bad at discomfort. I begin to feel that the world has deserted me, that things have fallen apart. I found the cold interesting, the way it moved in on me, but the bleakness immediately chimed with something mournful inside me. It returned me to the time when my mother used to take me out to, as she put it, 'walk the streets' while waiting to be evicted from our flat. As we walked she would tell me that this was how life was going to be now we were homeless. I remember watching my feet walk on the shiny wet pavement – we were in the Euston Road, having just failed to get rehoused at the Town Hall – with a vivid sense that once we were thrown out of the flat, there would be nowhere to go. It was a new notion, the idea of being on a street in London with no destination. It truly scared me. Sometimes I find myself in London at night looking for a taxi and fall, unreasonably, into a panic. I suppose it's a regurgitation of the 'nowhere to go' fear from those weeks when I was eleven. Suddenly, I am bereft, lost, and a terror wells up, for all that I am an adult in the centre of London with a centrally heated flat waiting for me not very far away. I've wept once or twice on the street, all of a sudden certain that no taxi will appear, all the buses will be full, just that I am out on the street and not securely at home. That's what happened on the beach at St Andrew's Bay. An irrational moment of pure unsheltered emptiness, and though my heart and everything else was already cold, it turned icier still with something more than the effects of windchill. Some things I'll never get away from, not even in the farthest reaches of the South Atlantic, but, with a bit of effort, I can recognize them as a passing wind blowing through me, chilling me to the bone, an act of nature that isn't personal, or not any more. If I wept on the beach at St Andrew's Bay, they were tears belonging to another time. The past can still make me shiver, but no bones are broken.

I walked on about half a mile, wending my way through crowds of penguins and avoiding the inevitable elephant seals, and was approaching the foot of the glacier when reality gave me a shout. The visit was being cut short. The ship had radioed that the windspeed was now sixty knots, almost twice the safety limit for the Zodiacs. Oddly, I resented being interrupted, low as my mood was. I badly wanted to get to the glacier; it wasn't home, but it was somewhere. By the time I got back, all but the last of the Zodiacs had started back for the ship. The final half dozen of us clambered back into the weather-swept dinghy and took a wild ride on a raging sea, which cheered me up no end. It took the driver a long time before he managed to manoeuvre us close enough to the ship for the sailor bouncing on the gangway to catch the rope and secure us. Butch waited as we staggered up the gangway, with a look of alarm on his face, until the last of us were back with both feet on the deck.

Delightfully, Daniel had opened the bar and prepared a hot rum and cream concoction which tasted so good my toes almost got warm. Marjorie and I adjourned to the sauna slightly tight, and giggled in the sizzling warmth about our wonderful afternoon out. Truly vanilla ice and hot chocolate sauce.

At supper I sat with a group of four American widows and divorcées in their sixties, doing Antarctica together. All but one managed to arrive with their hair perfectly coiffed and their trim, trained bodies looking decidedly *après-ski*. Only Barbara was unhappy. 'It was the worst experience of my life,' she wailed. 'The worst!' She couldn't eat with the memory of it. The cold had overwhelmed her and all she could think about was getting to bed and staying there for the rest of the journey. She was not upset, so much as outraged, by the weather, fear and discomfort. 'How could you do this to me?' she accused her fellow widows. When she left for her bunk, her friends discussed her neurotic nature, though quite affectionately. She was not in fact either a widow or a divorcée. She had never married.

'Oh,' said Joanie in a husky knowing voice, as slim, trim and merry a Texas widow as I'd ever seen, and definitely taken with Phoenix John as a prospect. 'That explains it.'

'But she's had affairs,' one of the others said in an attempt to redeem her.

Joanie shook her head and turned down the corners of her mouth. Clearly, Barbara had got it all wrong.

'What's the use of that?' she rasped, and we all shrieked with laughter.

More king penguins the next morning. Not so many this time, only 10,000 or so, but here, at the next bay along, Gold Harbour, there were chicks. Actually, they were more like rugby balls, in dense brown fur coats, or New Yorkers at Christmas time without the parcels. They looked elaborately cosy. I suppose they were covered in down, what with being birds, but the stuff looked so much like fur that I wasn't prepared to argue with my eyes. The chicks seemed to outnumber the adults, that were hardly bigger than their offspring and certainly more streamlined. Some of the older chicks were half-moulted, looking tatty and bedraggled, like bag-ladies. A few had only their heads and necks still covered in down so that, while their bodies looked sleekly black and white, like a proper penguin should, up top they were like small children in ill-fitting fur hats and mufflers.

The woes of parenting were there for all to see, though due to the latitude hardly anyone would. The chicks trilled incessantly at their parents who had arrived back from the sea with bellies full of krill. The nurturing adults seemed quite reluctant to part with it, only regurgitating it into their young ones' throats after much frantic bill stroking. The parents seemed much more interested in displaying to each other – or to my incorrigible eyes, complaining to each other – elongating their necks, stretching their beaks up to the heavens and shrieking like stricken folk. The noise – the trilling and shrieking of 10,000 birds getting and spending – was at the pain threshold. There was no snow here, just more volcanic rock and sand splattered with birdshit. The stench was also at pain threshold. The waste products of thousands of birds, squirting where they stood, produced a smell like no other I had experienced. While conservationists were worrying about the besmirching of pristine wilderness, I fought with my stomach to overcome the sour, fish-stinking fumes of this remote, unpolluted bay. Still not white, and certainly not peaceful.

The crossing was easy and sunlit, but as soon as we landed it grew cloudier and colder and the sky darkened with every moment. This was beginning to look like a rule for landings. Best not be anthropomorphic about the weather though, there was enough to be anthropomorphic about. Most of the penguins were standing ankle – or whatever serves in penguins for ankle – deep in a great pool of marshy water, while others lined either side of a rushing stream running down from the melting glacier in the cliffs above. At the back of the beach was an area of tussock grass and here gentoo penguins, smaller and plain black and white – your classic penguins – were sitting on eggs and building or rebuilding nests. They waddled about on muddy hillocks between the marsh trying to stay upright and hang on to their beakful of mud and loose grass. On a solitary mound of tussock grass sat a giant petrel on her nest, like a statue, alarmingly huge, quite unreal. A great, grey and white bird with a hooked beak the length of my lower arm, she swung her head this way and that, keeping each eye out for danger, though she seemed quite unconcerned about people approaching to take snaps. There was a tiny white head peaking out from underneath her massive undercarriage. It didn't move, its eyes were closed. Perhaps it was dead. Along the beach a complete seal skeleton lay at my feet ignored by the surrounding penguins. The bones and skull were perfect, the flippers intact, but the skin lay around the bones like a sleeping bag that had been unzipped and left where it had fallen.

Further along was a colony of elephant seals. As I approached, a massive bull mounted – or rather slumped himself on top of – a female who belched a noisy complaint at the intrusion but did not move. Somebody called out to me, and I turned to see an even larger bull coming from behind me, lolloping along at a strangely efficient speed, nose aflap and with something urgent on his mind. I got out of his way just in time. He didn't plan to hurt me, he would simply have run me down.

This was a world of single focus. The other bull, large enough, but smaller than the interloper, and with a less developed nose, skedaddled once the big beast was within a dozen feet. The monster bull took his rightful place on top of the female who showed no particular response, except to belch another futile complaint. The smaller bull shuffled away, turning from time to time with a sullen look. Those of us who witnessed this stood silently shaking our heads – the women, I mean; the men had an altogether different expression on their faces.

There was to be another landing that afternoon but Butch encountered a problem. We waited on deck while the big white hunter zoomed around on his Zodiac looking for a landing site at Cooper Bay, our final stop at South Georgia. He came back and announced that the planned landing beach was out of the question because it was full of fur seals, though he was off to find another with fewer seals along the coast. Fur seals are dangerous, it seemed. They move fast and attack people, especially as they were nursing right now. Butch explained to us that if confronted by a challenging fur seal, the trick is not to run like hell, but to hold our ground and display at them. This, he showed us, involved protruding our head and neck as far forward as we could and pushing our hands with splayed fingers out in front of us.

'That'll show 'em,' Marjorie muttered as the rest of us suppressed our smiles.

As we waited in line, a cowboy-boot-wearing Texan, travelling with his middle-aged child wife, turned to me.

'How're you? I'm a singer-songwriter,' he informed me.

'Merrill's the name, and this is my darlin' Billie. Ain't this the most exciting trip ever? Do you like music?'

I smiled hello to Billie, indicating that it was and I did.

'How about Hoagy Carmichael?' he asked, and tapping the rhythm out on the rail of the ship in the middle of the South Atlantic he looked into my eyes and crooned *Stardust*:

> *'Sometimes I wonder why*
> *I spend the lonely nights*
> *Dreaming of a song . . .'*

It was worth waiting half a lifetime and a trip to the end of the world for this moment, water- and wind-proofed from head to foot, rheumy-eyed and damp-nosed as I was. I joined in the verse:

> *'The melody haunts my memory . . .'*

'Weren't that great?' Merrill grinned.

'Really great,' I agreed.

'Here's my card. If you're ever in Texas, you come and see Billie and me. Don't forget, now.' He handed me a printed card from the pocket of his anorak. It read:

Merrill Moxon
Cowboy Songs – Cowboy Stories
Guitar & Vocals and
Sing-Along Entertainment

Having had my incongruous, perfect moment, and feeling I had waited long enough for Butch to return to tell us we could or couldn't go and see some more penguins, or more elephant seals, I began to brood about the pleasures of Cabin 532, Melville and my word-processor.

'I'm off,' I told Marjorie and went to the mud room to take off all I had put on, arriving back in my cabin with a sigh. I spent a satisfactory afternoon, sleeping, reading and writing. Marjorie and the others did eventually get to land. Butch returned, having found a fur seal-free beach, so their new-found seal-scaring techniques were never put to the test. But who knows when it might come in handy?

Dinner that evening was next to Irma. She was a young woman in her twenties who was travelling alone and had remained alone throughout the journey. She was distressingly thin, with a drawn, bad-tempered face, and her manner of dress was alarming: she wore baby-pink, bunny-fur sweaters and sweatshirts with cute cartoon animals embossed on them. Her long fair hair was tidied alice-band style with a pink or blue ribbon and on board she sported fluffy slippers. Her expression was always sour, in contrast to the sweetness of her colour scheme. She gave the impression of being an infinitely superior infant who wished to have no contact with anyone. So, naturally, I sat next to her for dinner.

She introduced herself languidly and explained that she was a post-graduate student, rather as if this excused her from further conversation with the rest of the table – we would doubtless not be able to sustain a dialogue with such as her.

Someone at the table mentioned that I was a writer. She looked amused and asked snootily if I had ever had anything published. When I replied – with equally infantile satisfaction – that I had, half a dozen novels actually, and she had established that these were real books published by real publishers, she turned her attention full on me, tuning out everyone else, and explained that she was writing a thesis on Conrad, and that there was a Conrad specialist in London by the name of X, had I heard of him? In fact, I knew him faintly. At which she looked a little worried and explained that she had been interrupted by certain personal problems and the thesis had been some ten years in the writing. She was not as young as the bunny fur suggested.

'I've come on this trip because, being Canadian, I felt it was important to go to the Arctic, as a matter of national solidarity. Then I was ill, but now I've spent my savings which were for the thesis, that's why it will take so long to finish, coming to the Antarctic because it's important to show solidarity with the planet. The ozone layer, you know?'

'Absolutely,' I said, though not convincingly because the rest of the meal proceeded in silence. We were eating steak that evening. Irma spent twenty minutes deeply concentrated on cutting her meat into perfect half-inch square cubes, trimming this inexact side and that with her knife and fork held like implements of dissection. When the task was completed she slid the cubes around the plate making empty spaces appear here and there as if some of the meat had been eaten. Then she neatly placed her knife and fork on the plate at six thirty precisely, wiped the tips of her pearly pink varnished fingernails and the pout of her mouth with a serviette, and said that she thought she would skip pudding since she had to go to her cabin to think about Conrad.

'Good evening,' she nodded regally to me, but to no one else at the table.

'Sleep well,' I replied.

'That girl ain't got the appetite of a bird,' observed Billie Moxon in a southern drawl, sitting opposite.

Merrill was deep in conversation with his next-door diner, explaining about being a Shriner.

'There was a kid in our town born with no hip. He weren't no Shriner nor nothing, but we collected money all the same to get him fixed. Now, when there's a big meeting, that kid's father feeds them all for free in gratitude.'

Now, blissfully, there were two more days sailing the empty ocean, as we left South Georgia to head along the Scotia Sea, down towards Paulet Island in the South Shetlands.

MRS ROSEN:	You were a very, very sweet little girl.
MR ROSEN:	You're still sweet.
ME:	Not sweet. Not me.
MRS ROSEN:	No, no, no, no – after what you've been through, my goodness. And later on, when we heard the rows, or heard of them . . .
ME:	Did you hear them?
MRS ROSEN:	It did affect you because you were totally full of nerves.
ME:	How do you mean?
MRS ROSEN:	Well . . .
MRS GOLD:	Fidgety.
MRS ROSEN:	Yes, it got to you. It got to you.
ME:	Twitching?
MRS GOLD:	Twitching, yes.
MRS ROSEN:	Yes.
ME:	I had all sorts of twitches.
MRS ROSEN:	Did you know that? I didn't want to say, but in fact . . . It affected you, because you didn't know where you were quite honestly. It must have been horrendous for you. Because I remember once

when you were on this floor, I got to the door, and your mother came out and said 'Oh, I've just hit him with a saucepan, or frying pan, and knocked him out.' I said 'Oh, my God.' She said 'I don't care if I've killed him.'

MRS GOLD: They were fighting.

MRS ROSEN: They'd had a fight. But after that, she didn't confide in any of us three.

ME: Did she try to put a good front on it?

MRS ROSEN: Yes. But she couldn't really, but as for the beginning, the early years, everything was lavished on you. The toys you had, the clothes you had. You had the best pram . . .

MRS GOLD: No, mine was the finest pram. Coach built, with initials on it. I learned what to do from someone in Great Portland Street.

MRS ROSEN: *Your* pram was the most expensive one. You had the best.

MRS LEVINE: Poshest.

MRS ROSEN: Yes, I mean, they lavished a lot of love on you at the time, but I don't know what happened. A clash of personalities, or just out to get each other . . .

ME: Do you think they were ever fond of each other?

MRS ROSEN: I don't know. Your father seemed a bit more sophisticated. Yes, well, she left her husband for him, so there must have been . . .

MRS LEVINE: Something.

MRS ROSEN: Yes, there must have been.

I was making life difficult for those women and the last remaining husband – apart from Mrs Gold who was as happy as a tick. This was my second visit and I was probably asking too much of them, especially Mrs Rosen who, though she understood that I wanted to know, was nevertheless uncomfortable about telling me about my family and my younger self. There was also a growing sense that she was becoming uneasy with an implied accusation that they hadn't helped. I felt uneasy about this as well. It was no intention of mine, no thought of mine, but a small cloud of censure did seem to hang in the air above the four of us taking tea again. It didn't feel like mine and I wanted it to disperse as much as Mrs Rosen did, but it darkened. I wasn't prepared to claim ownership of it, not even to myself, partly because it would get in the way of them telling me things, but also because I couldn't reasonably blame these people, getting on with their lives, landed with a dysfunctional family next door but one, for not doing anything about it. What could they have done? And if they chose not to notice our furniture being taken out, or my mother being carried away on a stretcher, who could blame them? I really couldn't. But clearly I did and I could sense a resentment that didn't quite belong to me, which was none the less mine. That cloud, like it or not, was something I had brought into the flat with me.

I tried to recall Jennifer feeling that they ought to be helping, and I couldn't. I didn't think she thought like that. I knew she thought that her circumstances were peculiar, they were like something from a story book rather than the real life she observed around her. I knew she felt trapped with the wrong people, that there was no way out of the small flat and her fighting family, but I didn't remember her ever thinking that someone around ought to do something about it. Or rather that anyone *could* do anything about it. Like me, I don't suppose she thought there was anything to be done except wait it out. That something was going to happen was part of the air she breathed. The suicide dramas, the fights, the death threats never quite came to a head, but it was clear that they would – had to – at some point. It was a matter of waiting for a cataclysm that would alter things. We all waited, my mother, my father and I for whatever it was that was going to happen.

Somewhere at the bottom of my private hankering for oblivion is the idea that it excludes waiting. Oblivion is a place that has no co-ordinates in time or space. Waiting would be impossible without future or destination. In the real world I dislike waiting, and at one time would do almost anything to avoid it. Making things happen was, perhaps still is, a way to subvert waiting. I learned to make things happen, or to prevent things from happening. I became adept at circumventing waiting, not by avoiding what was going to happen, but by making it happen now rather than later. Not exactly oblivion, but a release from the feeling of helplessness as the inevitable takes its time making its way towards you. In my dreams, though, I was after a state where nothing would or could happen. A condition where there was nothing to wait for. Call it a hospital, or a monk's cell, or a great, empty white continent. In *Moby Dick*, in the chapter on 'The Whiteness of the

Whale', Melville homes in on whiteness as absence and negation:

> Is it by its indefiniteness it shadows forth the heartless voids and immensities of the universe, and thus stabs us from behind with the thought of annihilation when beholding the white depths of the milky way? Or is it, that as in essence whiteness is not so much a colour as the visible absence of colour, and at the same time the concrete of all colours; is it for these reasons that there is such a dumb blankness, full of meaning, in a wide land-scape of snows – a colourless, all-colour of atheism from which we shrink?

Yes, probably – except that perhaps there is as much attraction as revulsion at such an absolute absence.

> And when we consider that other theory of the natural philosophers, that all other earthly hues – every stately or lovely emblazoning – the sweet tinges of sunset skies and woods; yea, and the gilded velvets of butterflies, and the butterfly cheeks of young girls; all these are but sub-tile deceits, not actually inherent in substances, but only laid on from without; so that all deified Nature absolutely paints like the harlot, whose allurements cover nothing but the charnel-house within and when we pro-ceed further and consider that the mystical cosmetic which produces every one of her hues, the great principle

181

of light, for ever remains white or colourless in itself, and if operating without medium upon matter, would touch all objects, even tulips and roses, with its own blank tinge – pondering all this, the palsied universe lies before us a leper; and like wilful travellers in Lapland, who refuse to wear coloured and colouring glasses upon their eyes, so the wretched infidel gazes himself blind at the monumental white shroud that wraps all the prospect around him. And of all these things the Albino whale was the symbol. Wonder ye then at the fiery hunt?

No, not really. What always seemed important – the only thing of importance – during a depression, was that I should see things as they really are. Depression is a lifting of the veil, what I saw when I was right down, was, I believed, what was actually there to be seen. Intolerable blankness. It could not be lived with long term, but from time to time I had to look at it, to know what was really there. When things looked better, I should keep a memory of how I had seen them in other, less protected moods. I thought that was vital. I still do. My attraction to blankness, to oblivion, was just as Melville described it, a sense that at source absence was everything. Colour was light and made the world livable in, but from time to time it was necessary to get to the blank reality. Depression is not good for one, it's an anguish I can do without. But the hunger for blankness could be assuaged, perhaps, in other ways. White walls, staring into peopleless landscapes, heading for the snow and ice. Not to stay, but to be in it for a while. Death,

182

of course, as Melville knows, is what it is. A toying with the void that finally toys with us. In the face of the waiting I can't escape, I head straight for its image and rest there for a while.

But for all my sense of not wanting to accuse the old people at Paramount Court, there is a phrase that lurks in the back of my head, which emerges from time to time in the whiny voice of a young child: 'Why doesn't someone help me?' I have been helped, of course, sometimes crucially, but still I hear it when I'm up against a blank wall. When I am sinking into a depression, when I'm stuck on a book, the phrase starts wafting around my brain. *Why isn't someone helping me? Why have I got to do this on my own. I can't.* There's a kind of comedy about this cross child unable to help herself who emerges from an adult woman who knows that the kind of help she wants isn't possible, isn't even desirable. A conversation ensues, the woman telling the child to shut up, that whatever it is can be dealt with and has to be. No one can sit through a depression for you and no one can write a book for you. *Why not?* yells the child. Because then you wouldn't have done it. *So what?* screams the child, stamping her foot. There's nothing to be done with this kid, but suppress her irrational demands. Tempting though, that *so what?* and not a question I've ever satisfactorily answered except with the eternal adult get-out of *Because!* 'Grow up' I mutter, but of course she can't, and I have, more or less, when not being challenged and tempted by the seductive question of my eternally angry child. That child is another me, still with me, as Jennifer is not.

But I do see that the child's outrage was reasonable once, and I wonder why Jennifer didn't stamp her foot and demand to know why someone reasonable wasn't taking care of things. I suppose Jennifer suppressed her, as I try to do now. Not so smart that, suppressing her then, not so appropriate. But what could the Rosens or anyone else trying to get on with their lives have done? I confess I did wonder what they felt later, when we had left the flats, whether they thought they should have helped. That child again, not Jennifer, or me; Jennifer and I couldn't for the life of us think how.

After the first visit to Mrs Rosen and her friends, I had thanked them, and though it surprised me, promised, as asked, not to use their real names in my book. I was very grateful to them for the effort. They are regular people, regular Jewish people at that, for whom scandal meant a good deal. It had been no plan of mine to eat their cake and drink their tea and make them say, as they did at times throughout the meeting, 'We don't ask. If people tell us, we'll listen, but we don't probe anybody . . . Nobody knew things were that desperate . . . I wasn't aware . . . Had we known . . . She wasn't that friendly . . . She wasn't actually a personal friend – well, at one time . . . I remember her going to hospital but we didn't know when or where . . .'

I didn't see, any more than they could, that they were in any way responsible for the disaster that happened to live nearby. I didn't go to see them to make them wonder what they could have done, but my presence alone must have done that.

'What more do you want to know?' asked Mrs Rosen when I phoned her a couple of weeks later and asked if I could see her again. 'We kept ourselves to ourselves. We don't know much.' It wasn't unkindly said, only defensive. I should have let it go, but I'd got home after the first meeting with them and spent several days in bed brooding. Not so much thinking about it, as shaken, as I hadn't expected to be, by the reality of my past in the reflection of their memories.

Jennifer, as story, suited me. I could look at her, think about her, even feel for her from the distance of a story-teller or historian. I deny *denial*, another word like *abuse*, that wraps up the complicated and in effect itself denies the texture of experience. If you want to know about toothache, it's necessary to have had one, but impossible to think about if you've got one at the time. Pain demands all your attention. If Jennifer and I merged, like the shadows of my mother and myself in the photograph, I wouldn't be able to see her at all. I wanted to get her into a better focus, not to become her. In any case, Jennifer was far more guarded than I am. I don't so much want to avoid feeling her underlying fear and unhappiness (I have access to that, in my own present way) as to avoid losing the already fragmentary recollection to a generalized emotional turbulence.

But I had been disturbed by Jennifer's new actuality. Mrs Rosen and the others talked about her as if she had been quite real. Their memories pictured her in the third person, as mine did, but their pictures were legitimate. I hadn't learned anything exactly new about my father, my mother, or Jennifer, but

I had heard it from the outside world, as recollection, not speculation. I'd learned that it was all, for want of a better word, true.

'You were a sweet little girl.'

Me. I was. Nerve-racking that. Not the sweetness, which was soon to be qualified by the twitching, but the fact that *I was*. Enough to send me to bed. Someone had been watching, it wasn't just me, myself and I waiting for it to end. I wasn't entirely a figment of my imagination, and up to that point, I could have been. They remembered Jennifer. Remembered me.

But it was fright that actually put me to bed. As I left that first meeting, I was shaken, shaking actually, with the information I had been given, not new, but readjusted, amplified. I knew that my parents were histrionic, but the slant on my father, not just a bit of a rogue, not just a bastard, as my mother said, but a professional con man, not just a bad husband and womanizer, but as inclined to suicide attempts as my mother, gave me a fright. Between nature and nurture it looked quite grim. I'd been, for some time, as I put it to myself, all right. But how all right could I be, genetically and psychologically, with parents like that? I came from a family of suicidal hysterics. I'd been suicidal and hysterical in my time, then taken stock and made a decision, or just grown out of it, but now I felt, as I walked back to the car, that I might not have the choice of being anything else; that for years I had been deluding myself into the notion that I had a choice. What sent me to bed was the thought – no, the conviction –

that I was the sum of those two people, that under the pretence of an achieved balance, more or less, I hadn't got a hope in hell of being other than what they were. I felt myself to have been all along skating over the thinnest sliver of ice; believing that it was solid when it was only ever a brittle and probably diminishing floe. My parents suddenly seemed inescapable, and I was caught up in the melodrama of feeling doomed. Thank you, Darwin; thank you, Freud.

I felt weak, fraudulent, and I could almost physically discern the flaky genes pumping around in my system, in my heart, my veins, my chemistry. I remembered very vividly how it was to give oneself up to emotional turmoil, to be at its mercy, to be unable to make any choices. I remembered that somewhere between Jennifer and me (each of us, in our way, able to deal with turmoil), there had been another one. Not the whining child who clearly was going to hang about until I was in my grave, but an intervening me, between Jennifer and my current self, who had turmoil and craziness at her fingertips; who had had years of training for the part and acted out what she knew best. I remembered now, while I was in bed, how truly immersed in doom I had been, how inescapable the craziness had seemed at the time. The one who in her early twenties lay between the white sheets, trying to keep them around her in spite of Sister Winniki's yanking at them, who was not in control, who had no choice. I could not then have pulled myself together, could not have chosen to get up and on with my life. I was quite will-less, it seemed to me then, to me now. Only nothing made sense to me; only nothing was worth fighting for. I was depressed, I would be depressed again; but later, however bad the depression, I knew I was in a particular place I couldn't get out of, but that other places existed. In my late teens and early twenties there was no other place in the universe to be in. I was all I could be, which was nothing striving for less. Or so I felt. I can remember being entirely out of my own control.

I had come to think of this period as a bad patch in my life, and the phrase 'acting out' belongs to my later self, forgiving and forgetting what I was like. But perhaps, I now thought, I wasn't exactly acting out anything, only being what I really was, what I couldn't help but be. I'd avoided acknowledging how authentic that version of me might have been.

My father's emotional vulnerability was far more concealed, at least from me, than my mother's. When I was still very small, he was as beguiling to me as he had been to the ladies of Paramount Court. I adored him; he adored me. At weekends the two of us would roam London, take possession of it. Saturday mornings watching the changing of the guards, patting the horses standing guard in the street, my father egged me on to try to make the guardsmen laugh. In the afternoon, we would explore the museums: the British Museum, or the museums in Exhibition Road, roaming the Natural History, Geology and Science museums, while he made up stories about the exhibits, ad-lib comedies that split my sides with laughter. *What a talker, such a charmer*, the old women had said, sighing. Sunday mornings at Petticoat Lane, buying pickled cucumbers, bagels and cream cheese, and then, after a Chinese lunch in Soho, an afternoon spent at the cinema, first at the news and cartoon house in the Charing Cross Road, and then to Leicester Square for a proper film, in the dark, the long tunnel of dusty light over our heads, his arm around me, my head against his shoulder.

Weekends were a glut. I was a glutton. We loved our weekends, we loved each other, and we laughed, as I recall it, from first thing Saturday morning until he put the key into the door on Sunday evening. Sometimes, if I played my cards right, I could get him to agree to go to yet another cartoon cinema before we finally went home. I knew he was always secretly pleased to be persuaded to do more, to put off ending the day. I delighted at being able to persuade him. Neither of us minded putting off having to go home to where my mother sat, not laughing, as likely as not with a headache, a giant box of prescription codeine close by her; or shut away, sullen, not speaking to us, in the bedroom; or, slamming down our supper – not hers, she had no appetite – spoiling for a fight, because it was inescapable that she was not nearly so loved as her husband and her child. London sparkled for us; our flat, when we returned to it, was as overcast as the industrial north.

He was a shelter against my mother. Strong, I thought. There was the time when the policeman came and told my mother about the fume-filled car, but that's a sharp momentary memory followed by mistiness. I can't remember how he was in that condition. I remember him angry, sulky, withholding. I

189

remember him violent – though in my recollection only in response to my mother's initial violence. I don't remember him vulnerable, except once. Mostly, I remember him making me laugh and being close. I knew he loved me, and even after he had left the last of several times without making contact with me, I knew he *had* loved me. Now, after visiting the old women, there was a new thought: I had been charmed by a man who made his living charming women. I saw myself suddenly as another of his conquests. *Anybody would be taken in . . . You had to love him*, the old people had said. This was a radical change of perspective; a brand-new loss. My father practising his skills on me. Some people cannot help but make people love them.

My mother's neurosis was never concealed. I'd never thought to appreciate that. She would lock herself away for days, sulk, not speak. She would accuse and curse. Her resentment and disappointment lived on the surface of her skin, trembling on her lips, glaring in her eyes, ready to flare at any moment. She wasn't well, as my father would comfort me after a scene. It suited both of us that my mother wasn't well and that, by implication, he was.

The first time I remember him leaving, I was about six or seven. 'He's gone, he's left,' my mother said. There's no way to convey the flatness, the despair in her words. You've heard it from time to time in the movie tones of Marlene Dietrich or Bette Davies. It was late, I'd been in bed for some time. I pretended to be asleep when she walked into the dark room and told me. I didn't know what to say, and I was frightened by what would happen to the voice if it was encouraged to go on. Besides, I had a despair of my own. He'd gone, he'd left.

It may have been the next day, or perhaps several days or weeks later, I can't remember, but I arrived home from school to find the bedroom door shut. My mother was often in bed.

MRS LEVINE: I had to go to work every morning. But on Thursday afternoons I was home and very often she would ring up. She was never dressed, she was never ever dressed. She would always open the door wrapped in a bathrobe . . .

MRS ROSEN: Once, I remember, I must have knocked on the door, she was wrapped in a bath sheet, and she'd probably been lying down in the dark. She suffered a lot from migraine, very bad migraine. She was depressed, I suppose.

ME: My mother often threatened suicide. Did she ever try?

MRS ROSEN: Not that I know of . . .

MRS GOLD: I think she did. She did. An overdose. How old were you? You'd have been five.

I opened the door to a daylight-darkened room, the curtains closed, lights off, an artificial dusk. There was a noise, a moaning, a weird wailing and I saw my mother lying in bed. She was naked, but she always slept naked. Only she wasn't asleep. She was rolling frantically from side to side in the bed, the covers in turmoil, like someone with a high-grade fever. Spittle dribbled from the corners of her mouth. All the while she was rambling. Talking to God, complaining about her life, crying 'Help me, help me', muttering maledictions.

I called 'Mummy' from the doorway, reluctant to go nearer, but she didn't answer, or notice that I was in the room, so I had to go closer to the bed.

'What's the matter?' I asked her, touching her clammy skin.

She flinched and stared wildly at me. A crazy woman.

'Don't you touch me,' she screamed. 'Who are you? Get out. I don't know you.'

Bad story-time again. She returned to her rolling and moaning at someone, perhaps God, perhaps not, invisibly in the room, but certainly not me. Not Jennifer, that is.

I don't really know what Jennifer felt. I don't remember her feeling anything. I suppose I must have been scared, who wouldn't be? I wonder if I wasn't also relieved to be unrecognized, not required to listen, dismissed. Now, I would feel relief; so what I remember is feeling nothing, just turning sharply to leave the flat, and business-like, ringing the bell on the door opposite. We didn't know them, but a woman answered the door and I said, politely 'My mother's ill, can you help, please?' A very practical kid. A bit of a cold fish, she must have thought when she entered the bedroom and found my mad mother writhing and keening in delirium.

Since then I've witnessed a good many people in various versions of mental ill-health, some of them extreme, but I've never seen anything quite like my mother's madness that day. It was almost too mad, too Grand Guignol to be true, it was just like madness is supposed to be, distracted, amnesiac, way-ward, as if Mrs Rochester and King Lear had come to life and tutored her. She was truly lost to the world. It was very mysterious, almost magical. For years I thought that this was what madness was. If you were mad, you lay in bed, reeling and writhing and rambling wildly and hadn't the faintest idea who your daughter was when she called you. Those were its symptoms, I thought, like a fever and sore throat were symptomatic of flu. I didn't think there was any other way to do it. When I got to a psychiatric hospital myself, aged fourteen, depressed but not demented, I was quite surprised at the variety I found.

They carried her off in a stretcher and someone in the flats, not Mrs Gold, Rosen or Levine, sent me to stay with a relative of theirs. Then I went to live with a family who I'd never met before, who it only lately occurred to me was a foster family, but who I was told were 'cousins'. I went to primary school nearby, wherever it was, and played with the other kids from the looming red block of flats, different from mine, a kind of tenement block, with, most wonderfully, an open lift that ran alongside the fire escape, like a dumb waiter in which we lethally zoomed up and down. Another game: hanging out of the bedroom window on the fourth or fifth floor with a torch and trying not to let the other kids catch the beam. I didn't like the foster mother, I got the impression she didn't like me much. I was not, by then, a very lovable child, but spiky and withdrawn. I took care to keep my distance, and if I longed for comfort and love I would under no circumstances ask for it.

There were several other children, most of them hers, I think. I remember feeling, for all the games, lost and strange. Wrong area, wrong flats, wrong people, wrong smells. At the same time, I didn't want to become used to this place and these people. I wanted to be where I belonged, though now I can't imagine where I thought that was. I took to sleep-walking every night, and the woman told me I had to stop it, how I might climb out of the window and, thinking I could fly, would fall to my death on the concrete below. I don't remember thinking about my mother, or my absent father. There was just the negative feeling of wrongness.

Then my father turned up. Out of the blue as far as I was concerned. He took me back to the flat in Paramount Court on that first visit, sat me on a dining chair and positioned himself on the floor in front of me, on his knees. He wept – this was the only time I saw his vulnerability and I hated it – begged my forgiveness, and made a solemn and formal promise through the tears – they dripped off the end of his nose to my exquisite embarrassment – that he would never, never leave me again. Then we went back to the tenement flats; he couldn't look after me himself yet, he told me.

After that he came once a week and we went not to Petticoat Lane, Exhibition Road or Leicester Square, but to visit my mother in the hospital. There was a lengthy bus ride and then what seemed a very long walk along a tree-lined suburban road. It was, I think, from a brief stay there many years later, Friern Barnet hospital, though it could have been Shenley which I half-recognized when I visited a friend in the mid-sixties.

Invariably during this walk I needed to pee, so each week we would knock at a different house and ask if I could use the bathroom. It became a game, a kind of roulette, a trip into uncharted territories. I discovered all manner of different toilets, and best of all, one with a musical toilet roll. We were never refused, and sometimes we ended up having a cup of tea with the householders. The charming father and his young daughter were given tea and biscuits by extraordinarily kind and trusting people who, while I was on the loo, were doubtless told of our visit to the ailing wife and mother in the mental hospital up the road. I suppose they thought it was a shame, and such a nice man, poor child. Those brief visits belonged to the realm of our earlier museum wanderings; the house and people, the exhibits; our meeting people and seeing how they lived, like the stories my father used to make up about the things in glass cases. They were adventures into unknown worlds, people whose houses, whose lives looked to me so solid and stable. Settled houses for real families with chintz-covered furniture that had the quality of eternity about it, and silver-plated teapots, waiting in glass cupboards and brought out for visitors. Other lives. But frozen by a single visit into comfortable certainty. It was like going to the movies, too, and slipping through the light beams into the lives on the screen.

Until, of course, the reason for our being there could be put off no longer and, for me, the price of being with my father had to be paid for by seeing my mother. She was inaccessible for a long time, months, I think. We would be taken to her side room by a nurse and find her sitting blankly on her bed. She didn't know us from Adam and couldn't have cared less. She wasn't dramatically mad any more, she was a shell now, an emptiness, either drugged or semi-catatonic, or both, which passively received our bunch of flowers from the nurse who took them from my hand and made approving noises as she placed them on my mother's lap, where they lay pointlessly until the nurse more practically went off with them to find a vase.

Once, during a depression, when my then seven-year-old was taken care of by her father, I tried to explain to her that she wasn't to worry, it wasn't about her, but a difficulty all my own, an illness I got sometimes, and that it would pass. 'I'm not worried,' she said, coolly. 'I just need you.' I felt quite encouraged by the clarity of this.

I wasn't worried by my mother's depression, either. I don't think I cared, or had anxiety about my mother's condition, but I don't remember knowing that I needed her. I wanted familiarity, to be in circumstances I knew, but emotionally I was as absent, I think, as she was. I didn't want to see her, or sit with her and make the pointless conversation my father tried to encourage, while she stared balefully ahead. I was no more interested in her than she was in me. But she hadn't been a neglectful mother; erratic, demanding, alarming, but not neglectful. She was devoted to me, to how I looked, to what I ate, to my progress at school. How I appeared, how I did were signs for her, telling her how she was doing in the world. And perhaps she loved me. I don't know. I know that she thought that having a child guaranteed that she would be

196

loved. That was what she found so unnatural and unsatisfactory about me. Sometimes she said, 'I have to love you, you are my daughter.' Love was obligation, and in saying that she was reminding me of my obligation to her. I always found it less than satisfactory. I would have preferred to have been loved for some reason, some quality other than accident of birth. But very likely, she meant what most people mean when they talk about the unconditional love of parents for children. It was a kind of assurance, but somehow it didn't assure me. She even had a story, not thousands like my father, but just one which she told me at bedtime if my father wasn't back, or when I was ill and she sat through the night with me and my fever. It was a version of *The Water Babies* without the water, but with Tom the boy chimney sweep befriended by a girl, by Jennifer, who took care of him and saved him from his wicked chimney sweep father. I relished this story in which I was the hero, and always wanted to hear it. This is the warmth I remember with my mother, when I make a special effort not to deny her her emotional rights, but though I know I loved to be told the story, I can't think of it as anything other than an exception to the general anxiety and unhappiness I knew with her. It wasn't enough, at any rate, to make me feel I needed her when she was mentally absent. I was, as my mother had frequently and accurately told me, quite heartless about her.

It seemed, however, that only with my mother's recovery was I going to get my father back. We would 'all live together again' my father assured me, when my mother got better. And it would be different, he said, there wouldn't be the terrible rows, and he would never leave me again. I'm sure it was put in terms of leaving me, and not my mother. Even the 'better' it was going to be was to do with my well-being, rather than any stated new feelings for my mother. In the meantime, I had to stay with the foster parents because he couldn't look after me by himself. I'm not sure how much I believed this new story of my father's. I loved him, but I suspect that by then, even before then, I didn't quite trust him. He painted a picture of cloud-cuckoo-land, pretty but insubstantial, as all the stories were. But if I didn't have any real faith in the story, I liked it and participated in it.

MRS LEVINE: He had a wonderful way.
MRS GOLD: He was a handsome man. Very handsome. A ladies' man.
MRS LEVINE: He could talk anybody into anything. He had that personality, the way he spoke, you had to listen to him.

There was a need, after all: I needed my mother to get better, so that I could have my father back full-time.

There was an odd incident when I was very small. On my third birthday, my parents took me to see Danny Kaye at the Palladium. We sat near the front and he saw me, asked me to go up on stage and sang a song to me. During the interval I was taken round to his dressing-room, where I sat on his lap and drank my first Coke. He enchanted me, with his kindness, funnyness and solidity. I felt he loved me. One day, some time later, while I was walking with my father through the West End I was suddenly overcome with longing for Danny Kaye. More than anything in the world, more than the moon and the stars, more than the whole world, I wanted him to be my father. I walked along holding the hand of my actual father, who I adored, but was consumed with the need to have this other father I had known only for a few minutes. I began to cry at the tragedy, as I suddenly perceived, that Danny Kaye never could be my father. That the thing was fixed. The crying gathered pace, and I became convulsed with sobbing grief. My father picked me up and tried to find out what the matter was. This only made it worse because suddenly I felt that I had betrayed him by wanting another father. I couldn't tell him what the matter was, but I couldn't stop mourning my loss. Things were so bad that several cars stopped at the kerb and offered my father a lift, thinking I had been taken ill. I cried all the way home and cried myself to sleep without telling anyone what the matter was. This is one of the most vivid memories I have as a small child.

There is another that my adult self has connected to that memory of longing for a different father, and the guilt I felt. It must have been around the same time. I was very small, two or three, and I was woken from sleep by a particularly violent shouting match between my parents. I went into the other room and stood in the doorway. When they saw me they stopped and my father asked me what was wrong. I asked why they were shouting.

'We aren't shouting,' he explained. 'You don't understand. Sometimes grownups have conversations when they talk very loud. There's nothing wrong, dear. Just go to bed.'

I knew he was lying. I suppose it was the first lie I knew about. I remember the shock, and not arguing but going back to bed, pretending that I believed him. I loved my father more than I could say, but I don't think I really believed what he told me after that.

It took a while but eventually my mother started to know who we were when we visited the hospital, and managed a limp smile at our arrival. Soon, there were stiff, nerve-racking little visits to a back room of a local tea shop, and an occasion when both my mother and my father came and had tea with me at the foster woman's house. When we all went to live back in the flat, it was explained to me that Mummy was very fragile and I must be very careful about what I said. In fact I always had been, but now the surface of the world itself had turned to delicate ice and we all tiptoed over it, my mother, too, pretending that everything was all right now. It didn't last long. Things returned to normal within a few months. The fights and the silences between them that sometimes lasted for weeks, returned, though now we had moved upstairs to a flat with another room – my own room – but it soon became my mother's retreat when the rows came to a pitch and it was door-slamming time.

My father took me by the shoulders one day when I was almost eleven and nearly finished at primary school. He told me that he was leaving for good. I was unprepared for this. I hadn't noticed that things were any worse than usual. 'This time, I'm never coming back. Do you want to come with me, or stay with Mummy?' It was a straightforward question that required an immediate answer. His bags were packed and standing by the door. I have no idea why, except that I didn't know where he was going, but I said with hardly a pause that I would stay with my mother. The decision remains a mystery, but I suppose it's reaching to call it a decision. It was more like a nervous reaction to a sudden announcement that life was going to change again, and the nonsensical requirement that I state my preference there and then for good and all. My preference had always been for my father. I chose to stay with my mother, and watched him disappear through the door with his suitcases. Perhaps I thought it was what a girl should do. Perhaps I didn't want to pack my bags and head off for the unknown. I don't know why.

He disappeared from our life, except for my mother's diatribes against him. No word, no money. Just gone. Except once when we saw him at Tottenham Court Road tube station and my mother chased him with the knife she kept in her handbag expressly for the purpose of killing him should they ever meet by chance. He outran her.

For a while a tall thin man was in the flat a great deal. He had been going to redecorate the flat when my father disappeared and flat decoration became an idle dream. He wasn't decorating. Then he wasn't there any more. A woman turned up – in her forties, perhaps – at the flat to find my father. She was from Denmark and had tracked him down, intent on finding the man who had apparently romanced her mother, a woman of sixty plus, out of her small income. She seemed to feel sorry for us and gave me ten shillings before she left. This was useful because there was no income, with my mother unable and unwilling to work and refusing to go on social security. By then, the rent not having been paid since my father left, we were just sitting around waiting for eviction.

Waiting again. For weeks we lived in the empty flat while my mother sat helplessly in the armchair the bailiffs had left, telling me that when they finally came and threw us out we would go and live on the street – under the arches of Charing Cross, to be precise. We would practise, she said as she dragged me by the arm and whisked us out of the flat as if we were never going to return. 'What's the point of waiting to be thrown out? Now, we're on the streets. This is it. We're homeless.' I remember it as always raining on these occasions. Probably, it wasn't always raining.

This time I couldn't stand the uncertainty. I had just started at grammar school, and went every day as if nothing unusual was happening. 'Don't say anything to anyone,' my mother instructed. 'If anyone asks about your father, say he's dead.' I did as I was told. Better a dead father than to admit to desertion. I wondered how I was going to manage going to school when we were living under the arches. I failed, repeatedly, to arrive at maths lessons with a geometry set. The cost was out of the question. I didn't even mention it to my mother. But every day at the beginning of maths I had to stand up and confess that I still didn't have a geometry set. It became a class joke, whipped up by the archetypal sarcasm of the maths mistress. One morning, instead of leaving the flat and going to school, I lay down on the floorboards and started to scream. I refused to go to school again. Two weeks later the social workers arrived, alerted to my non-attendance at school. I'd short-circuited the waiting.

ME: It must have been a scandal when the bailiffs came and seized the furniture.

MRS ROSEN: I just heard about it. I just heard.

MRS GOLD: I just thought she left. No, I don't remember. You were there one day and then you'd gone.

MRS ROSEN: After you'd gone nobody knew what happened. Nobody knew where you went.

MRS GOLD: After your father went, your mother had this builder . . .

MRS ROSEN: A scandal, I remember a scandal. He was always there.

MR ROSEN: It was unheard of.

MRS GOLD: It didn't last long because you left.

MRS ROSEN: There was so much going on in this building, it wasn't such a big issue. Please believe me. Your mother and father, the builder, it was part of everyday life that was going on. We all had children.

MRS GOLD: So you were on this floor when you left?

ME: Yes.

MRS LEVINE: Oh, they weren't the only ones who did a fly-by-night from this floor. A couple, with a little girl, on this floor . . . Sadly, the daughter has not made it like Jennifer has. She was in bands. She came into Harrod's and she looked like a beatnik. Black eye make-up and earrings. And he wrote a book on horses. The husband was away and lover boy . . . and this one and that one . . .

'What more do you want to know?' asked Mrs Rosen at the beginning of my second visit to Paramount Court.

I wanted to know what I had forgotten to ask about the first time.

'I wonder how you remember me as a child.'

I think she was quite relieved at discovering that I didn't want her to tell me more about my parents and her relationship with them.

'You were a very, very sweet little girl . . .'

I had had the best pram in town, or second best if Mrs Gold is to be believed, and my clothes were the best money could buy.

MRS ROSEN: They lavished a lot of love on you at the time, when you were very little, but I don't know what happened there. You were very clever when you were a child. How did you get so educated? When you phoned out of the blue, I was thrilled to hear you'd done so well, with your start. I'll never forget that first day you went to school. You were tiny. You had this little grey hat and a grey uniform. You were always tiny and dainty.

MRS GOLD: You had a fourth-year birthday party, they made for you. It was the party of the year. All the kids went home with better presents than you got. You had lavish parties when you were young. Must have been money there.

MRS LEVINE: Your mother did have some jewellery from her first husband. For a while . . .

MRS ROSEN: As a child you were very bright. You were the youngest of all our kids. You were the baby. But you were up to it. You were the cleverest. What they did, you could do, maybe better. You could talk! You could argue! You kept up with them. You could stand up to the others. You always knew how to stand up for yourself.

Mrs Rosen, with innate kindness, was giving me what I wanted: a telling of me, a story for me about the me I didn't know or recall. I thought of browsing through Chloe's photograph album with her when she was younger. She'd say: tell me about this, what was I like then, as she examined photos of an infant and toddler she doesn't remember. Over the years we have told and retold her childhood for her. A photo, a story, a flickering memory, and Chloe, like all of us, regains her past in a patchwork story that becomes whole cloth of a sort. It's not untrue; or it's as true as cameras, fleeting moments, and my memory, along with my side of the story, can make it. I've watched Chloe's memory being built out of clues and recollections. Tell me again about the cheesecake, Chloe would ask, and a bright, fidgety, social toddler is summoned up, wandering around a restaurant, charming the other diners, empowered by her childishness to provoke friendliness and affection in strangers, until over-excited, she knocks over one child-resistant woman's cheesecake and discovers that charm and childhood does not always guarantee that people will adore her. How shocked she was, when she returned to our table, at having encountered a stranger's anger. Roger and I had to tell her the story over and over again for months, while she digested the complex reality of the world out there, and her first social catastrophe. Now, she doesn't consciously remember either the cheesecake moment, or the constant retelling of it, but she does remember it through our re-remembering together. False memory? Just memory.

How did my mother remake my unremembered life for me? We had a photo album, too. There were photos of me as a baby and I would gaze at them, while the album still existed, trying to make the remote creature real. 'You were so lovely when you were a baby. When you were asleep. Like an angel. Then you'd wake up and turn into a devil.' This was affectionate, a pleasing joke my mother and I had between us. What else? Nothing I can remember. Just the baby photo and the joke about being asleep. More regularly, when she wasn't joking or telling me *The Water Babies* story, when despair and disappointment were uppermost, she would refer to my infancy with 'If I'd known how you were going to turn out, I'd have strangled you at birth.' And, 'You were always rotten – like him. Even as a baby you were incapable of love.' No baby pictures of these moments, except my own internal ones.

There was a real atavistic, mother-and-child moment of satisfaction for me when Mrs Rosen offered me four-year-old Jennifer standing up for herself. It passed, but still the picture of obdurate, unputdownable Jennifer, aged four, pleased me. It also chimed with other memories of my childhood. Mostly they were memories of being in trouble, of refusing to back down, of demanding my rights. There was a tough child, right from the start, with a sense of herself. A survivor. I remember often being scared but refusing to let it show. I suspect that for all the difficulty this trait got me into over the years it may also have saved my life. Since then I may have split my selves into manageable parts, but back then, and all along, there may have been some continuing consciousness that knew exactly who and what it was, and remained solid in that knowledge. Sometimes I am ashamed of this survivor. Some less positive aspect of myself dislikes the degree of will, the determination it implies. But the fact was, there was this survivor to put against the flaky genes and the training in hopelessness. I suppose, with the threat of my live or dead mother suddenly coming back into my life, I had gone to Mrs Rosen to find out just that. To check that there had once been and always was that survivor. And Mrs Rosen, inadvertently or not, gave her to me in an unexpected moment of good mothering.

The next morning around 6.15, I lay shivery in my bunk, with a sore throat. I had a streaming, screaming head cold and felt ghastly, but it was OK since it was a travelling day and I didn't have to do anything if I didn't want to. I had woken earlier, at four, to the unrelenting daylight with a small damp weight inside of me. A tiny blueness. Perhaps it was a moment of panic at being out of reach of anywhere, hundreds of miles out of sight of land. A kind of bleakness. I closed the beige curtains across the bed, making a soft half-light, enclosing myself, and dozed on and off.

Later, I got my achey self up to look out of my window. Birds: pintados, petrels, black-browed albatross (I was getting good at this) were wheeling around, dipping and diving on the wind to feast off Melville's 'effulgent Antarctic sea'. The surface of the water was dark, hardly lively, but active enough to create a gentle rocking motion in the boat that sent me back to bed to enjoy it. I carried on with *Moby Dick* and Ahab's search for the great white whale. Such a pleasure. Grand, huge and free. Taking all the freedom a novelist needs. I couldn't think of a circumstance that would improve my life – apart from not having a cold. Though soon I would have to get up to have breakfast – which meant other people, greeting, smiling and talking. That felt like a bit of a trial. My wish was to stay where I was, in my cabin, in bed. As I put my book down for a moment, I looked through the window and realized that it was snowing. The sky was dove grey with heavy snow-weighted cloud, and the snow was falling softly, making the windswept wilderness of the Antarctic sea as silent as any suburban winter garden. The horizon was a very long way away.

I skipped breakfast and both of the lectures designed to help fill our at-sea time, devoting the day to my cold, my bunk, my book and the view from my window. I was perfectly contented. Sleeping, reading and staring out at the snow and sea, I could have done this forever. No Sister Winniki to nag. Just left alone to take all the pleasure I wanted in indolence. What more could anyone want?

Then in the evening the first iceberg floated by.

The iceberg emerged before my lazy gaze at the window, like a mirage, a dream appearance, a matt-white edifice ghostly in the misty grey light and falling snow. A sudden, smoothly gliding event in the great empty sea under the great empty sky. I blinked at it. There was none of the disappointing familiarity of something seen too often on TV or in picture books. This startled with its brand-new reality, with its quality of not-like-anything-else. Even the birds seemed to have hushed for our entrance into the land of ice. The tannoy squawked into life, and Butch announced:

'Ladies and gentlemen, we have icebergs.'

209

Time to get up. I pulled on a tracksuit and headed up to the bridge where I discovered that like a momentous theatrical production we were proceeding into real Antarctica through a corridor of icebergs. For as far as the eye could see, to either side of us, icebergs lined our route. We were journeying along iceberg alley. It was absurdly symmetrical, like a boulevard in space. The bergs were tabular; as their name suggests they are flat as a table on top, as if someone has planed away their peaks, too smooth to be real, too real to be true. It took about an hour before we had sailed the length of iceberg alley, and all the time I and many of the other passengers stood and watched in silence, broken only by gasped oohs and ahhs and the inevitable camera clicks and camcorder whirr. For a while after that we seemed to travel through debris, odd-shaped bergy bits, and the larger growlers – some just the dimension of buoys bobbing and rocking like corks in the waves, others the size of a dinghy or a small cottage. These were the remnants of big bergs, worn down by wind and water, breaking off and melting away eventually to nothing. Finally we sailed through cracked pieces of ice, chips and fragments, as if we were making our way through a bowl of granita.

Later, in the early hours of the morning, more big bergs appeared, not in formation any more, but dotted about on the sea in gatherings of two and three, some of them huge, the size of our ship and bigger. I watched one go past that, we were told the next morning, was four miles long, an island of ice that took an age to sail along.

I didn't get much sleep. Irma may not have been so patho-
logical in her attitude towards the steak. I was feeling
decidedly nauseous and having stomach cramps. The light-
soaked night was spent divided between hovering over my
toilet without quite throwing up (there is very little I hate
more than vomiting), and leaning out of the open window
with my chin on my folded arms watching the superlunary
white mountains float by. Sometimes, as I watched one huge
berg sailing towards us, it would shift shape, playing parallax
games, and getting nearer, became two or three separate bergs
at what I finally saw were a considerable distance apart. Then
when we had left it behind, it returned again to its singular
form.

As a matter of fact, in keeping with the interesting but not
fatal disparity between my fantasies and rest of the trip so far,
the icebergs close up, even quite far away, were not daydream
white at all. Blue. Icebergs are blue. At their bluest, they are
the colour of David Hockney swimming pools, Californian
blue, neon blue, Daz blue-whiteness blue, sometimes even
indigo. Blue is an odd colour: the signifier of good things to
come ('blue skies, nothing but blue skies') and of dark
thoughts ('Mood Indigo'). Different shades, different promises, same colour. It can be bright, clean, even cold; and it can
be mysterious, deep, the colour of night and dreams. Like
Melville's notion of whiteness, it makes clear and it obscures;
it is purity and complexity. The colour blue does no violence
to my hankering for white. It belonged with and in the ice,
making it seem colder, emotionally empty, and yet more

dense, layered beyond what could be observed. The bergs were deepest blue at sea level, and where cracks and crevices gave a view of the depths of the berg where the ice was the oldest and so compacted that all the air had been forced out. Why this should cause them to be aching blue is not a question that someone who spent physics lessons turning notes into poetry can answer. The blue tinge higher up was, I was told, because ice absorbs all wavelengths of light except the shorter blue ones. I told this proudly to Marjorie who pointed out that this account would cover the reason why anything looks any colour. Melville again: there is no colour, only an appearance of colour that conceals the universal negation of white light. The explanation didn't after all explain anything much, and once again I wished I hadn't dicked around during physics and deprived myself of answers to most of the questions I now found myself asking.

These floating mountains of blue ice shaded with white, white ice shaded blue, were not slick and shiny like ice-rink ice. They were dense, matt islands of compressed icing sugar. Confections that lit up the lead-coloured sea and sky. All night they floated along, carved by wind and water into ancient shapes – ships, castles, monuments, mythic creatures. None of the explorers who described them managed to avoid these descriptions. They are as unavoidable as a sigh at the sight of the elephant seals having sex. I passed great craggy faces in profile, ominous fingers pointing, lions crouching, birds leaping. The mind couldn't help it. But sometimes, and most breathtakingly, they were simply vast walls of ice, passing so near to my window that they cut out the rest of the world. A great blank wall of ancient compacted snow that had travelled from the blank centre of the Antarctic continent for centuries – the deepest ice is 10,000 years old – to its edges to become a tongue of glacier or the very periphery of the ice cap, and finally broken off – calved is the correct term – to sail away on its own. They head north and west at a rate of five miles a day until they reach the convergence where the Antarctic Ocean meets warmer seas. Some of them last for ten years, until the sea erodes and melts them away.

Antarctica has seventy per cent of the world's fresh water locked up in the ice. In places the ice sheet is two and a half miles deep. Over the centuries people have planned to utilize the bigger icebergs as a source of water in drought-stricken regions. The only problem has been how to get the bergs from where they are to where they're needed. Grandiose plans to tow them have come to nothing: once they are into warmer water the chances of landing more than enough ice to cool a gin and tonic are unreasonably small. Icebergs are one resource that the human race has failed to find a way to make use of – apart from Daniel and my Manhattans. While the sea ice, pack-ice, frazil, nilas, pancake-ice are salt – though not as salt as sea water – the bergs that break off from the continent are pure fresh water – as pure and fresh as anything can be on the planet. Certainly, for all the pollution, purer than the stuff that comes out of our taps. And these mountains of frozen water I watched floating on the surface of the sea are, as everyone knows, just the tip of the iceberg. Nine-tenths of each berg is indeed below the waterline, and melts faster than the bit you can see, so that eventually they become top-heavy and turn turtle into the sea. The smaller, most rounded bergs are actually upside down, tip-turned and unstable. Growlers, they are called, and not loved by sailors; they are the ones that creep up and scuttle ships in the dark, being harder to see and often invisible to radar.

The scene from my cabin window was otherworldly, I am afraid there is no other really apposite description. In the early hours of the morning, the light was pale silver, slightly misty. Half-close my eyes and there was nothing but a spectrum of grey, blue and off-white. It could have been bluey grey, greyish blue, hues of blue. There were huge bergs coming now. I suppose they were related. They came in waves. Three, four, but no, they were two big bergs. They must have broken off at the same time, or it could have been one great berg that split. On the horizon the cloud seemed to have settled down on to the sea and turned into another iceberg. It was impossible to tell what was cloud and what was berg in the distance. It looked fluffy, the same colour as the clouds higher up, only distinct, and squat, flat on the sea, but still cloudlike for all that. But it wasn't a cloud. Soon it turned into one . . . two separate bergs. It was all clouds and bergs, bergs and clouds. And there, close by the ship, was a single penguin on an iceberg that looked like a lion. The bird was riding on the lion's mane, standing stark still, looking ahead in the direction in which it travelled. I'd never seen a penguin look heroic before. It was 3.20 a.m. and luminous, misty daylight.

We stopped off at Deception Island, making the approach after breakfast, in silvery light. The name alone was worth getting up for. Who would want to lie abed when they were sailing towards Deception? The sight from the bridge was immortal. Deception Island is a caldera, a volcano summit that has collapsed to form a crater. One section sank far enough to allow the sea water to flood into the interior of the caldera. As we approached 'Neptune's Bellows' at the entrance to the crater, fleets of penguins came out to see what we were and swam, ducking and diving, alongside the ship. The sea was veneered with a pattern of sea ice made up of perfectly sharp-edged rectangles that looked as thin as wafers and pure white, floating side by side with narrow channels of dark water in between. It was a chessboard of flat floating squares of ice, as strange and orderly as anything I'd ever seen. It was shocking when the ship broke through one of the bigger rectangles on its way to the narrow entrance to Deception. The bow of the ship split the ice floe into two pieces which grew jaggedly ever wider apart as we pressed on through. There was something terrible about this, about breaking up the pattern just because we wanted to get beyond it. No real damage was done, but something artful in nature was dislocated. The design was spoiled. And yet the further into the checkerboard we got the more we seemed to be part of it. Soon it was surrounding us, an abstract picture made with great but delicate four-cornered slabs of ice, floating in the hazy sunlight, with a small white ship slipping through. The Zodiacs went ashore but I remained on board, on the deck at the back of the boat, and stared all morning at the chequered ocean. Checkmate.

The following morning I woke, still feeling rotten. Everything ached, my head was thick and I still felt sick and crampy. I couldn't move, not even to take a pill, not even to check out the state of the icebergs. I'd been up and down all night, at the window, then dozing, until I finally went back to sleep at 6.30 and slept until late. It was 11 a.m. and as light as it had been in the early hours. It was always light now, we were so far south. The lack of alternating dark and light made it very easy for me to stay where I was. The call to breakfast, lunch and the time-passing lectures failed to intrude on the structureless nature of continual daylight and feeling ill.

What was going to happen to my Antarctic adventure if I sank for days into my bunk, I wondered? Unless, of course, this *was* my Antarctic adventure. I was quite suspicious of my malaise. Through the aches and the nausea, pleasure shone through, at escaping the timetable, the events, the socializing. I guessed it was probably my psyche, rather than my immune system, that had revolted against being snuggled in with so many people. Still, the psyche had effectively persuaded the body to produce some impressive symptoms – good enough to justify hermiting without having to accuse myself of being anti-social. Though I did, in fact, accuse myself.

We were coming into Admiralty Bay, where humpback whales were supposed to hang out. We hadn't sighted any whales so far. Well, I could look out of the window if there were any sightings. Though only if they happened to be on my side of the ship. But I didn't want to see whales with a whole bunch of people on the bridge or the deck. I didn't want to be in a crowd watching whales, even if it meant missing them. I wanted to see my own whale out of my own window, all by myself. Or not. I imagined explaining to friends on my return to England how I didn't manage to see a whale. Wrong side of the ship. Didn't get up. Oh dear.

The following morning we were due to land at Paulet Island. Outside it looked very weird and alien. I had to keep telling myself I was on the same planet. Not on the moon. Maybe this sickness or not-sickness (I'd managed to throw up some yellow bile that night, which made me feel a little more authentic) was panic at not escaping, at never escaping. Here we were at the end of the earth and still it's the same planet. I would have liked to get somewhere else. Further off. One morning I was alarmed at being out of sight of the world, the next I was blue about not being able to escape the world altogether. Not very consistent, I told myself. Myself shrugged. I wondered, at last, if I was going to prevent myself from landing on Antarctica. What an odd thing, to have come all this way and then not land on the peninsula. There was a small but unmistakable internal smile at the thought. I located a tight subterranean knot of unwillingness to set foot on the last continent just because I happened to be there. Though of course I didn't just happen to be there. This was a place where no one just happens to be. Which made it all the more pleasing and/or distressing (the

217

two emotions were inextricable) to consider the possibility of not stepping on to the land. There was considerable satisfaction at the thought that I might not set foot on the continent that I had taken a good deal of trouble to get to. I considered further ventures: how I might fail to let the sand run through my fingers in the Gobi desert; how I could turn back twenty-five feet from the summit of Anapurna; how, gaining disguised entrance to a Masonic initiation ceremony, I would shrug my shoulders at the door and wander away. I could easily go to Agra and fail to clap eyes on the Taj Mahal – too easily. What about a trip to Brazil spent entirely in the air-conditioned confines of the Brasilia Sheraton? Or a visit to every airport in Africa without setting foot on the continent itself? I could keep myself busy as the resistant traveller until my last gasp and then, at the gates of Heaven, make my excuses and turn away. It's not the arriving but the not-arriving . . . it's not the seeing of the whales, but the possibility of choosing not to see them. This was an aspect of me that I recognized from every period in my life. The Fuck-it Factor. *I don't have to if I don't want to.* Sometimes it has looked like a lack of persistence. 'What you lack, my girl, is stickability' my oh-so-resolute father would say to me. I didn't finish pictures, knitting, stamp collections. Lost interest two-thirds, or even nine-tenths of the way through. I got thrown out of school. I left school two weeks before my A-levels. I wandered away from relationships. Sometimes, even now, I turn off movies on TV minutes before the end. Lots of people have nodded knowingly to each other, 'She just can't finish things'. But no one ever mentions the exhilaration of

218

not finishing things. The rush of pleasure at not doing what is
expected of you, of not doing what you expect of yourself. Of
not doing. If it was originally about disappointing other people,
it has become refined into a matter of pleasing myself. Of
making choice less inevitable. But it's not a policy. Only something I notice happening from time to time, and the genuine
satisfaction that goes with it. This time I'd caught myself in the
early stages. Unless, of course, I was just not well. You can't
say, and I may not choose to say.

I became gripped by the idea of willingness. As I gazed
out of the window, I imagined myself into the future: the trip
over, me back in London. Did I or didn't I get to Antarctica?
At that delicious moment I really didn't know what the answer
would be. It wouldn't make an iota of difference to the world,
or in reality to me, if I didn't actually stand on the Antarctic
landmass. Been there, haven't done that. I liked the absurdity
of it, and the privacy. It's a matter entirely between me and
myself. Indeed, I could say, back home, that I did, when I
didn't. What difference would it make? Or, come to think of
it, I could say that I didn't, when I did. And once I'd had this
thought, it didn't matter whether I actually did or I didn't.
The quality of my life wouldn't alter one bit, and either way
only I, and a handful of fellow travellers, would know, and
none of us would care. The decision became entirely aca-
demic. I could toss a coin: heads I land, tails I stay in my
bunk – and then not go if it comes up heads. Or contrariwise.
I might not have been feeling well, but my spirit was soaring.
There was no longer a choice that had to be made, or an effort

of will (I should, I ought, I must), no moral quandary, but something quite arbitrary. A great sense of freedom settled gently over me like a pure white goose-down quilt, and freedom, from that angle, looked very like uncertainty, as Antarctica slipped into Schrödinger's box and closed the lid quietly on itself. I had no idea whether I would get up and land the next day or not. And no one else, save a few scattered US citizens, would know for sure what I eventually did. This, for reasons I don't choose to examine too closely, was a huge comfort. What was all this getting to Antarctica thing anyway?

The book I was going to write about the trip, and my mother, was to be my first full-length non-fiction, it had been agreed. I took this to mean that I would not be writing a novel about it. Obviously. Who would agree to write a novel about a real trip they hadn't yet been on? Novels aren't like that. But beyond that I reserved my judgement on what non-fiction is. There are infinite ways of telling the truth, including fiction, and infinite ways of evading the truth, including non-fiction. The truth or otherwise of a book about Antarctica and my mother, I saw from my swaying bunk in Cabin 532, didn't depend on arriving at a destination. Nor in failing to arrive. I found myself beginning to get a taste for non-fiction.

Another day, and the tannoy announced that we were as far south as we were going to get: 63.42S 55.57W. We had arrived in the early hours at the Antarctic Sound. My landing quandary was resolved for this morning at least. The pack-ice was too thick to get through to Paulet Island, and things weren't looking good for the landing on the Peninsula at Hope Bay, scheduled for the afternoon. It looked possible that no one would be landing on Antarctica, and my decision – as so often – would be no decision at all in the event. However, Butch was doing his best for us and had arranged, instead of a walkabout on Paulet, a Zodiac cruise around the great field of icebergs surrounding us. The sun was blazing beyond my window and the sea was glacially still. There wasn't a ripple to be seen on the turquoise surface, nothing but the sharp reflections of the bergs. Suddenly, I thought I might be feeling a bit better. Time to get up. I very much wanted to get close up to the icing sugar mountains, and down near the surface of the brilliant sea.

After my sullen, anti-social couple of days in my cabin, I found myself greeted in the corridors, in the mud-room and on deck by everyone I saw, welcoming me back and asking how I was. They had noticed I was not around and asked Marjorie and Phoenix John if I was OK. I felt a little ashamed at the concern people were showing for me. Part of my sense of shame was that I slightly resented their attention. I don't like the idea of being thought or wondered about if I have gone to ground. This was so ungenerous compared to people I hardly knew telling me they were glad to see me up and about, that I was not pleased with myself.

The only noise was the buzz of the Zodiac engine. There was no wind, no screaming penguins, and when the Zodiac stopped at the foot of an iceberg, no sound at all, except for water lapping against the wall of ice. The sun shone and the sea was a deep green with sparkling lights, twinkling like sequins. The surface was calm, just slightly wrinkled by the gentle breeze, almost syrupy. A Crimplene ocean. Between the bergs, so common now but never boring, were flat ice floes, slabs several feet thick, on which the odd crab-eater seal lolled soaking up the sun. So long as we didn't get too near they refused to be bothered by our pottering about. If we went too close they slithered unhurriedly into the sea and disappeared.

To be at the base of an iceberg, rocking on the sea, is a remarkable feeling. The cold radiated off the wall of the berg and I peered into secret crevices that went to the deepest blue heart of the ice. The world was flat and still except for the bergs ranged above us as we wove in and out between them. The ship at anchor, as white and still as another berg, belonged there, another mythic shape in the landscape and didn't seem to impose itself. It was uncanny and peaceful, a near oblivion, but deceptive. This was not a place, though it was a position on a navigation chart. Nothing about this region would be quite the same again, as the floes and bergs floated and melted, winds whipped up the presently calm sea, seals made temporary lodging, and flotillas of penguins porpoised around the ship in the distance like flying fish. Everything about this seascape would change, but it would also remain essentially the same, its elements merely rejigged. It was so untroubled by itself that the heart ached. Other landscapes fidget – rainforests full of plants and creatures clamouring for a living, moors troubled and ruffled by scathing, distorting winds, mountains trembling with the weight of snow – but this was truly a dream place where melting and movement seemed only to increase immutability. Nothing there stays the same, but nothing changes.

But what, I wondered, was the point of witnessing this sublime empty landscape and then passing on? That question was one reason, I suppose, for the rate at which the cameras clicked away. The photograph was evidence for oneself, not others really, that you'd been there. The only proof that anything had once happened beyond an attack of imagination and fallible memory. It also caused there to be an event during the moment of experiencing, as if the moment of experiencing doesn't feel like enough all by itself. If you merely looked and left, what, when you returned home, was the point of having been? It was not hard to imagine such a landscape, to build one in your head in the comfort of your own home, and spend unrestricted time there all alone. In real life, you look, you pass through, you leave – you take a photo to make the activity less absurd. It provides something to do with your hands while you are trying to experience yourself experiencing this experience. But how do you become, as I wanted to be, part of this landscape, to be of it, not making a quick tour through it? What I was doing was having a taster of something, watching the trailer of a movie I would never see. I would take this memory of a place in motionless flux back with me, and add it to the Antarctic in my mind. I wondered

223

if it would be a useful addition once the experience was in the past.

But I had forgotten about Cabin 532. That *had* been a new experience, something I hadn't already dreamed up or dreamed of, somewhere I couldn't have visited through pictures taken by someone else. Cabin 532 was something really new to carry back to London and play with.

The will to live was not strong in my family. I had my own version of it, which I had developed into a passion for oblivion. It began in earnest at fourteen when I discovered that sniffing ether stolen from the chemistry laboratory at school put me out for what seemed like several lifetimes, although I was assured when I came round that I had only been unconscious for a couple of minutes. This elongation of existential emptiness was a delight to me. The ether was one of the reasons I was expelled.

When I took my mother's Nembutal in her room in Hove it was because I wanted everything to stop. I had no definite thought about killing myself, only of stopping everything – same result but different feeling. Later, after I left school in the late sixties and started taking whatever drugs were around, what gave me most pleasure was to inject dissolved Nembutal directly into my veins. This had the effect of rendering me instantly and utterly unconscious. Only years later did it occur to me that this was a very bizarre way to have fun, but it wasn't really fun I was after, it was nothingness. Between my mother's Nembutal and my own I spent some time in the psychiatric hospitals being treated for depression, but what they were for me were places of safety, blank places of white sheets and nothing happening. Actually, life in the bin was vivid, things happening, dramas constantly, but hermetically sealed within the world of the hospital. Life itself – the business of getting and doing, of *participating* – was on hold, which was where I wanted it to be. I didn't have to do anything about day-to-day living. The hospitals were convents for escapees from life; enclosed, safe and with their own rules for disengagement. I and the other patients were inmates, intensely close in a conspiracy to lock out the world of our regular lives. We lived entirely with each other, anyone outside was an intruder who had no right to enter our existence. We looked after and protected each other from outside visitors and relatives exhorting us to 'get better'. Even Sister Winniki was preferable to getting on with living. I did not want to function, to live my own life, to achieve anything. I only wanted to be let alone.

Being depressed is very painful, but it is also silence and absence. There is a paradox. The pain, real anguish, is intolerable. I would do almost anything not to experience it, but the silence and absence of the place where depression puts you brings the possibility of getting close to contentment. This is not to say that I had any conscious control over depression, only that I discovered that sometimes, if I sat through the pain, I got to a place of absolute peace and quiet. This is not a statement of the value of depression. Depression is rotten, you cannot sit through the pain if your circumstances aren't right, if you haven't got support, or if you have people depending on you. And even if those conditions can somehow be met, to sit through the pain carries the very real risk that you will not survive it. But given that depression happened to me, and I did have support, I found it was possible after a time to achieve a kind of joy totally disconnected from the world. I wanted to be unavailable and in that place without the pain. I still want it. It is coloured white and filled with a singing silence. It is an endless ice rink. It is antarctic.

The week before I returned from Antarctica Chloe had gone off for a fortnight to South Africa with her dad. The house was empty when I got home. I like the silence of an empty flat after I've been away, it gives a chance to repossess the place. On top of the piles of post on the kitchen table was a note from Chloe saying she'd opened anything interesting-looking, and it turned out nothing was. On my desk in the study was a small pile of papers topped by another note from Chloe. 'About your mum and dad – I went to Hove with Dad to your mum's house.'

Hove was where my mother had last lived, where I had last lived with her for just two days, after I had run away from my father and Pam in Banbury.

Chloe had been busy while I was away. On top of the pile were some certificates. The first was my father's birth certificate. He was born on 15th October 1908 in Bethnal Green and named Israel, the son of Sam and Golda Zimmerman. Sam having just arrived from Poland was still a journeyman furrier, and his name was signed in what must be Hebrew and annotated underneath by the Registrar: 'The signature of Sam

Zimmerman, father.' Beneath this was a death certificate announcing the death of James Simmonds, fifty-seven years, a sales representative, in Banbury. He died of myocardial infarction and ventricular fibrillation on 20th April 1966.

It's hard for me to assess what kind of a journey it was from Israel Zimmerman, Sam Zimmerman's son, to James Simmonds, but it doesn't seem to have been one worth making. I know that my father was a disappointed man, but I'm not sure he was disappointed for very good reasons. I have a letter of his, written to me when I was sixteen and living in London, having been sent back to school to do my O-levels by the woman who invited me to live with her. He was in Banbury with plain, dull but devoted Pam, the woman who, when I had lived with him, he had twice tried to swop for someone more exciting but failed, returning to ensure himself of domestic comfort at least. It was just a year or so before he died. He complains that I don't write frequently enough:

For good or ill, I'm the only father you'll ever have darling, so make the best of a not very good job.

I'm very glad to hear Mummy is passing through a sensible phase – may it last this time.

How is your work dear? Are you doing any writing? I toyed for a while with the notion of having a bash at an autobiographical novel, but I can't find the incentive. Like most things – it just ain't worth it! Yet what could Errol Flynn write that I couldn't better?

Sobering thought. Much love, Dad

He used to mention Errol Flynn a lot towards the end of his life, how the rakish movie star's adventures were nothing on his. Usually this was said rather glumly from the depths of a chintz armchair in the sitting room in Banbury. Reality wasn't a strong point with my dad. Another letter written at this time, just after I had clearly visited him and Pam reluctantly for a weekend in Banbury. The letter reads in part:

I was very glad to see you at the weekend, but somehow I have the feeling – very strongly – that you were not very happy to be here. This impression began as soon as you arrived, and didn't change when I left you.

Is there so little point of contact left between us now? Can you no longer find any satisfaction in being with me, and regarding my home as yours too?

However self-sufficient you feel yourself to be, there will be many times when you will feel the need for your own family and a place to call your own. What are you trying to prove? Self-sufficiency? That's nonsense because everyone needs someone at some time or other.

He goes on to complain that I am improvident and smoke too much. Both undoubtedly true.

I have decided that it will be better for you if I do not send you your usual pocket money, but will bank it for you and then buy Premium Bonds which will be difficult for you to spend. I hope it will mean that you will buy

fewer cigarettes, and enjoy the fruits in greater financial
security. Do try to be sensible dear. Love, Dad.

My father was a fantasist, but towards the end of his life the
dreams had become domesticated, recuperative. They were
unwarranted – for him – fantasies of family commitment and
social responsibility. I read his letters and blinked at the surprising notion of domestic normality they seemed to spring
from. I wouldn't have minded being the difficult, smoking
and improvident teenager with baffled loving parents not
understanding why I should have become so troublesome.
He'd walked out, leaving us penniless, when I was eleven and
only come back into my life because I found him. I lived with
him and Pam briefly in silence and anger at the transformation
of my father. At one point he met someone else and he and I
went to live together in a flat. When the new relationship
failed, he told me it had been because of me, because I hadn't
been affectionate enough to the new woman. We went back to
Pam with me in disgrace. Having asked to go back to boarding
school, and got expelled, I was not allowed to return to school
('I've done many bad things in my time, Jenny, but I was
never sacked from school'). Now, his fancy of good if distant
fatherhood at this late stage in our relationship rendered down
to teaching me to be aware of the value of money ('Although
you have had lots of reason to know this for yourself, you are
still improvident' his letter had said), and worrying about my
smoking. It was like watching a man pretending he was standing with his family on the top of a cliff when we had already

long since fallen to the bottom. I didn't like the lies he told himself, but I could see why he had to. What I resented was the loss of the man who had made me laugh so much. That man had disappeared into thin air, so utterly that I had to wonder if he ever existed. His dreams had become so dull, so pompous. I never told him that, I just shrugged the letters away.

Not long after receiving that letter, a year before he died, he took me out to lunch and handed me an envelope which was not to be opened until he had gone back to Banbury. I went to the loo and read the letter. It was a suicide note (*'By the time you read this…'*), enclosing the log book for his car, which I would receive as soon as his estate was sorted out, and details of his life insurance policy, the proceeds of which were to come to me *'on Pam's demise'*. He simply informed me of his forthcoming suicide, giving no reasons beyond not being able to stand it any more. The main point of the letter was to get straight what I would and wouldn't inherit.

I returned to the table, frozen, said nothing, barely breathed until he left, and then went to jelly. I had just let him go, not mentioned the letter, pretended I hadn't read it. I hadn't even tried to stop him. I was put to bed, a weeping heap. When I called his number the following day, he answered the phone, sounded jovial, never mentioned the letter. Neither did I. I cut off contact with him. Then he died of a heart attack.

There was another certificate in the sheaf of papers left for me by Chloe. It stated that Rachel Simmonds, otherwise Rene

Simmonds, maiden name unknown, had died on 28th March
1988 at the Royal Sussex Hospital, Brighton. The cause of
death was a) subdural haemorrhage, b) carcinomatosis and c)
carcinoma of the pancreas. Somebody called Betty Young had
reported the death officially and caused the body to be cre-
mated. The last address of the deceased was 3 Third Avenue,
Hove, East Sussex.

My mother was dead, but what struck me most forcefully, as
I put the certificate on top of the pile, was the thought that she
had been alive for twenty years after the time I had last seen
her. That is, *been alive* all that time while I had been living my
life. Been alive when I was in the bin, doing drugs, being a regular teacher, having my daughter, publishing my first two
books. She had been in Hove that day I went to Brighton with
Chloe and made jokes about running away from mad old
ladies. It was as if the painting of my past had acquired a
shadow, a new presence, separate but lurking darkly around
corners in doorways. Not that she would have known anything
about me, my name had changed, but she had been *there*, in the
world, living and breathing in parallel with me and my doings.
The death certificate confirmed, most immediately and most
shockingly, not her death, but her existence up to 1988. It
wasn't that I had been certain that she was dead, only that in
uncertainty she had stopped existing for me. But she hadn't
stopped existing. She'd been around all along. Living, breathing, thinking. And instantly the past looked darker and more
cluttered than I had pictured it up to then. There had been the
possibility all along up to 1988, the retrospective possibility,

that she might have made contact; might, as in my worst early hours anxiety, have turned up in my life. She hadn't; she might have. Only for the last eight years had she truly not existed; only since 1988 had I been really orphaned, truly safe.

Finding her last address on the death certificate, Chloe had gone off sleuthing with Roger to Hove. The bottom pages in the pile were her description, typed up for me, of what she had found out:

> ### Three Third Avenue, Hove
> Flat 3: Thomas someone, the caretaker
> Flat 4: Rene Simmonds
> Flat 6: John T.
> Flat 8: Bill E.
> Flat 11: Weirdo Washer-upper

This intro had the pleasing distance of a play. Pinter, perhaps. It continued:

> The road is wide, when we went there everything looked grey, but a light bright grey, with blue sea at the end. A very large, darkish building, though not quite bleak because the windows are too big and the bricks are not dark and dirty enough. Probably Victorian. I was surprised by its location, look out of the front window to your right, about two hundred metres and you see the sea. Rene's flat didn't face that way.

The intimacy of that 'Rene' was startling. I used to wonder from time to time what I would call her if she did turn up again. 'Mummy' was out of the question. 'Rene' wouldn't have done either, it might have indicated that I was ready to take her on, to look after her. Perhaps, I'd concluded, I'd call her Mrs Simmonds, the name, it turned out, she had held on to until the end. Mrs Simmonds had a nice, distant, non-committal ring about it. And it wasn't my name. Then I'd shake the conundrum away, reassuring myself that she wasn't going to turn up. But Chloe seemed to have made some relationship with her during her search, though I was happy to see it wasn't close enough to call her Granny.

The door was left open. I think some students were moving into Flat 2, downstairs. Flat 4 is immediately opposite the front door and to be honest it didn't really connect in me that she had lived behind it. I was too busy trying to get hold of the other tenants and playing Sherlock. We tried all the bells from the bottom, there were eleven or twelve, and none of them answered until we got to 6. John T. didn't act amazingly surprised by our mention of the name, and was happy to have us talk to him, and asked whether we'd like to come up or him down. We went up. Can't remember the smell, I guess not that striking, probably musty. Large staircase, getting darker, but it has a feeling of the grandiose that all those Victorian buildings try to create (they do it better in the larger ones). Maybe that's just how I see it, I always get that feeling when I go into old big houses of any sort. I would have liked it a lot if I was younger. But it is shabby and gloomy really.

I enjoyed the detail in all this. I remembered the gloominess. Not in that actual house, but wherever it was that she lived when I was there.

There are two bedsits on each level. At these landings there is a walled construction and the two doors are behind this. Flat 6 was on the far side of the building, and John opened the door as we arrived. He is a poet. His room is small and messy, with books and stuff everywhere, and when I think of it now I see it as beige. He probably lived alone, but there is a younger man with him. He is in his sixties with a ponytail. He has a tired and what you would call an interesting face, and has a roll-up hanging out of his mouth. He is a bit grimy, and is nice, but odd. He is a publisher of poetry. There are lots of Stephen King novels, but unless he throws his books away, his bookcase is fairly small for a literary person, but he probably goes to libraries. There is a filing cabinet marked 'Poetry'. Not overly friendly, but probably clever, he guessed my curiosity as a sentimental granddaughter wasn't the only motive (that is, he said he had after I told him you might write a book). He thought we were poets wanting publishing. Anyway once I told him about the book, he gave me a knowing smile and said 'I can understand, being involved in literature myself.' But although he knew Rene, they weren't close. She was very withdrawn, he said. Some of the tenants at 3rd Avenue lived in another road. The house was made into a solicitor's office so they all moved here. Rene lived in her old bedsit (the one you knew) with a man called Jack. He died about one or two years before the big move. She also had a friend called Jean. But she died around the same time as Rene. She never mentioned you or your father to John T. We had stayed about ten minutes and most of the time he was saying 'I wish I could tell you more, but I don't know anything else about her' or words to that effect.

I imagine Jack was the man who visited me in the hospital. She lived with him, then. Well, I was glad she wasn't alone. Did I mind that she never mentioned me to John T.? I noticed it. So perhaps she put all that, me and my father, her bad luck, behind her. Perhaps she had made a real life for herself with Jack.

We didn't know whether to go to Flat 8's door or ring the bell. We decided just to knock, but we had to wait a very long time for the man to answer – I think he was a bit scared. Once Bill E. opened the door and saw me it was all right. I think he felt safer with me, because he kept looking at me, not Dad. We didn't go into Bill's flat, we just stood in the doorway. He has longish grey hair, a tooth missing and a piercing stare, but seems nice. I was very aware of the crazed behind doors, each one I met was not quite right, but they are just normal people. He knew more. Said your mother and Jack were always at each other's throats, the house shook with their fights.

Ahh, no change after all. This Rene began to come more clearly into view as the woman I once knew. My mother and Jack, always at each other's throats in the house of the not-quite-right. Making the best and the worst of things.

But after Jack died 'she lost the will to live . . . nothing to live for . . . isolated . . .' I guess she had no one and didn't want anything to do with anyone. Bill said he once had a conversation with her about her ex-husband and she fondly recalled a romance in Paris. That's all. He thinks they might have had something to do with an antique (junk) business – where was the money to live? He also remembered that she was in hospital a few times. He mentioned that the caretaker in Flat 3 might have some more information, as he had cleared the flat after she died. There was no answer at his flat, but we left a note with your number, explaining what we wanted. He hasn't rung back.

Well, there was my father. And Paris? She always had Paris. I wonder if she was in the same hospital as me, or was it phys-ical ill health, perhaps when they discovered her tumour? Cancer of the pancreas. Well, why not? People have to die of something. Most people die of cancer.

Onwards to Flat 11, which John had suggested as he was
in the great move of, I guess, the mid-eighties. Didn't get
an answer at his door, but there was enough evidence to
see what kind of man lurked behind it. There were two
things stuck to his door: a postcard of neon kicking legs in
high heels reflected in mirrors, and a biblical quotation
about being welcome, hand-written with words added
above the main script – either his own, or he had made a
mistake or two. We could hear sounds of furious washing
up. We banged a lot. I don't know if this man was closest
to Rene, from what you've said he seems strange enough
to be – maybe he's the one we really should be speaking
to. Who knows. But we gave up then. Went downstairs,
smiled at the students with their boxes, and left.

I was glad Chloe gave up on the manic washer-upper with
the postcard legs and biblical misquotation. I'd had enough of
the house of the not-quite-right, as she clearly had. We both
got the picture. And there it was. My mother firmly dead, the
unknown remains of her life lived in a gloomy house in Hove,
fighting with a man and remembering Paris. Nothing really
had changed.

Chloe called from South Africa the next day.
  'Are you upset?'
  'No. Yes. Disturbed.'
  'Not surprised. But at least she didn't turn out to be some
sweet old lady who everyone loved. I was worried she might. It

was a bit of a relief to hear she went on being the way you told me she was.'

'Me too.'

Chloe was right that it was a relief to know that my version of my mother had been corroborated. Maybe I had got it twisted, or perhaps she had blossomed into a life, people change – it was shabby of me, but I was relieved to hear that she hadn't. The house still shuddered with the fighting, and when the man she fought with died she lost the will to live.

It was terrible in a way that I should be so relieved to find that she had remained just as I had remembered her – that she had been as I had remembered her. Not fair on her, as ever. But as I began to read Chloe's notes I had a sharp moment of anxiety that everything I recalled, everything I had told my daughter, might have been imagined, fantasized, fictioned. Or that, having got rid of a wicked and ungrateful daughter, she might have become another, renewed, fulfilled person. How would I have felt about that? Pleased for her, if I was halfway decent. But I'm not. I chose to prefer to discover that I had not been lying to myself and Chloe about her. I preferred my mother's continued unhappiness to finding myself to have been deluded all these years.

'Sad about her losing the will to live, though,' Chloe said.

'Yes, but what Bill E. didn't know was that my mother lost the will to live three times a week. It was a habit with her.'

'Will you go to Hove?'

'No.'

'Will you write to the caretaker?'

239

'No.'

'But you're pleased I went?'

'Very. Very pleased. Thank you.'

'That's OK. Good to know about your mother at last, eh?'

'Mmm. Yes, I think it is.'

STRANGER ON A TRAIN
Jenny Diski

'We were on a train, out of the way of our lives, any of us could tell anything we liked. We were, for the time being, just the story we told.'

In spite of the fact that her idea of travel is to stay home with the phone off the hook, Jenny Diski takes a trip around the perimeter of the USA by train. Somewhat reluctantly she meets all kinds of characters, all bursting with stories to tell, and finds herself brooding about the marvellously familiar landscape of America, half-known already through film and television. Like the pulse of the train over the rails, the theme of the dying pleasures of smoking thrums through the book, along with reflections on the condition of solitude and the nature of friendship and memories triggered by her past time in psychiatric hospitals.

'Funny, poignant and beautifully written . . . the result is, amongst other things, a profound and unsettling account of alienation' *Peter Parker presenting the J.R. Ackerley Award for Autobiography to Jenny Diski*

AFTER THESE THINGS
Jenny Diski

After These Things is an account of the relationship between Abraham's tragic son Isaac and Isaac's son Jacob. The book follows the psychological trail of the children of Abraham, the first properly constituted family, and finds that, like all families, their story is one of wishes and fears. In Isaac and Jacob's relationship we see all the complexities of love, power and desire that make them quintessentially human.

The inimitable Jenny Diski tells this ancient story anew, with the deliciously subversive wit and intelligence readers have come to expect from this wonderfully surprising writer.

'Seizes the story of Jacob and Esau by the throat and subjects it to an energetic process of what one is tempted to call energetic rehydration. She takes the desiccated fragments of those texts and drops them into her own fluid imagination, where they bloom, miraculously, like so many Japanese paper flowers . . . Goodness, it is interesting. And all it took was Diski's cool, elegant, rather cruel prose' *Sunday Telegraph*

A VIEW FROM THE BED AND OTHER OBSERVATIONS
Jenny Diski

'As a general rule I try to maintain a balanced and realistic approach to life. I'm convinced that the best place for a rabbit's foot is at the end of a rabbit's leg. And if there are fairies at the bottom of the garden, they go about their business and I go about mine.'

This is a wonderfully animated collection of Diski's essays from sources including the *London Review of Books*, the *Guardian*, *New Statesman* and the *Observer*. In her inimitable style, coupled with her sharp wit and idiosyncratic views, Disk reviews her own experiences, an array of key historical figures and pertinent topics. Ranging from 'The Sexual Life of Catherine M.' and her ponderings on the thrill of guilt, to the biblical role of water in 'Did jesus walk on water because he couldn't swim?' this is vintage Diski.

'Diski . . . is always sharp and witty with a lavish range of cultural reference' *Daily Mail*

'She is intelligent, funny and challenging' *Independent*

Now you can order superb titles directly from Virago

☐ After These Things	Jenny Diski	£14.99
☐ A View from the Bed and Other Observations	Jenny Diski	£8.99
☐ Nothing Natural	Jenny Diski	£6.99
☐ Only Human	Jenny Diski	£6.99
☐ Stranger on a Train	Jenny Diski	£7.99

The prices shown above are correct at time of going to press. However, the publishers reserve the right to increase prices on covers from those previously advertised, without further notice.

Virago

Please allow for postage and packing: **Free UK delivery.**
Europe: add 25% of retail price; Rest of World: 45% of retail price.

To order any of the above or any other Virago titles, please call our credit card orderline or fill in this coupon and send/fax it to:

Virago, PO Box 121, Kettering, Northants NN14 4ZQ
Fax: 01832 733076   Tel: 01832 737526
Email: aspenhouse@FSBDial.co.uk

☐ I enclose a UK bank cheque made payable to Virago for £ . . . .
☐ Please charge £ . . . . . . to my Visa/Access/Mastercard/Eurocard

Expiry Date ☐☐☐☐   Switch Issue No. ☐☐

NAME (BLOCK LETTERS please) . . . .

ADDRESS . . . .

. . . .

. . . .

Postcode . . . . Telephone . . . .

Signature . . . .

Please allow 28 days for delivery within the UK. Offer subject to price and availability.

Please do not send any further mailings from companies carefully selected by Virago ☐